Brilliant Windows Microsoft® 7 for the Over 50s

Joli Ballew

Prentice Hall
is an imprint of

PEARSON

Harlow, England • London • New York • Boston • San Francisco • Toronto • Sydney • Singapore • Hong Kong
Tokyo • Seoul • Taipei • New Delhi • Cape Town • Madrid • Mexico City • Amsterdam • Munich • Paris • Milan

Pearson Education Limited
Edinburgh Gate
Harlow CM20 2JE
United Kingdom
Tel: +44 (0)1279 623623
Fax: +44 (0)1279 431059
Website: www.pearsoned.co.uk

First published in Great Britain in 2009

ISBN: 978-0-273-72915-0

British Library Cataloguing-in-Publication Data
A catalogue record for this book can be obtained from the British Library

Library of Congress Cataloging-in-Publication Data
Ballew, Joli.
  Brilliant Microsoft Windows 7 for the over 50s / Joli Ballew.
      p. cm.
  Includes bibliographical references and index.
  ISBN 978-0-273-72915-0 (pbk. : alk. paper)
  1. Microsoft Windows (Computer file) 2. Operating systems (Computers) I. Title.
  QA76.76.O63B359227 2010
  005.4'46--dc22
                              2009035725

10 9 8 7 6 5 4 3 2 1
13 12 11 10 09

Typeset in 11pt Arial Condensed by 30
Printed and bound in Great Britain by Ashford Colour Press, Gosport, Hants

The publisher's policy is to use paper manufactured from sustainable forests.

Brilliant guides

What you need to know and how to do it

When you're working on your computer and come up against a problem that you're unsure how to solve, or want to accomplish something in an application that you aren't sure how to do, where do you look? Manuals and traditional training guides are usually too big and unwieldy and are intended to be used as end-to-end training resources, making it hard to get to the info you need right away without having to wade through pages of background information that you just don't need at that moment – and helplines are rarely that helpful!

Brilliant guides have been developed to allow you to find the info you need easily and without fuss and guide you through the task using a highly visual, step-by-step approach – providing exactly what you need to know when you need it!

Brilliant guides provide the quick easy-to-access information that you need, using a table of contents and troubleshooting guide to help you find exactly what you need to know, and then presenting each task in a visual manner. Numbered steps guide you through each task or problem, using numerous screenshots to illustrate each step. Added features include 'See also...' boxes that point you to related tasks and information in the book, while 'Did you know?...' sections alert you to relevant expert tips, tricks and advice to further expand your skills and knowledge.

In addition to covering all major office PC applications, and related computing subjects, the *Brilliant* series also contains titles that will help you in every aspect of your working life, such as writing the perfect CV, answering the toughest interview questions and moving on in your career.

Brilliant guides are the light at the end of the tunnel when you are faced with any minor or major task.

Publisher's acknowledgements

The author and publisher would like to thank the following for permission to reproduce the material in this book:

Microsoft product screen shots reprinted with permission from Microsoft Corporation.

Every effort has been made to obtain necessary permission with reference to copyright material. In some instances we have been unable to trace the owners of copyright material and we would appreciate any information that would enable us to do so.

Author's acknowledgements

The older I get and the more books I write, the more people there are to thank and acknowledge. I am thankful for many things, including the opportunities offered by Pearson Education every time there's a new Windows edition, and the awesome team of editors and typesetters who work tirelessly to turn my words into pages and those pages into books.

I am thankful that I have a supportive family, including Jennifer, Andrew, Dad and Cosmo. I am thankful to my extended family for all playing a role in my daughter's upbringing and success. I am thankful for my health, much to the credit of my doctor, Kyle Molen. Between the lot of them, they keep me in check, on track, healthy and sometimes even sound.

I miss my mother, who passed away in February of 2009, but I am thankful that someday I'll be able to see and talk to her again, something she worked hard to make me understand shortly after she passed away.

And finally, I'm thankful to my agent, Neil Salkind, who encourages me, is my biggest fan and who always has my back, no matter what. Everyone should have someone like that in their lives.

About the author

Joli Ballew is a Microsoft MVP, a college instructor and author of over 30 books, many for Pearson Education. Joli enjoys all things technical and is always branching out into new territory. Joli enjoys working in her garden, reading and watching disaster movies on the Science Fiction channel, as time allows. You can contact Joli anytime at Joli_ballew@hotmail.com

Dedication

For Mom, I miss you deeply.

Contents

Introduction

i

Welcome to *Brilliant Microsoft® Windows 7 for the Over 50s*, a visual quick-reference book that shows you how to master all of the features of the new MS 7 OS. Specifically written for those of you who did not have significant contact with computers in your working lives, but who now have the time to explore the possibilities of new technology. Fully updated throughout to cover MS 7 it provides an easy-to-use guide to anyone wanting to get the most out of their computer.

Find what you need to know – when you need it

You don't have to read this book in any particular order. We've designed the book so that you can jump in, get the information you need and jump out. To find the information that you need, just look in the table of contents or Troubleshooting guide, and turn to the page listed. Read the main text, follow the step-by-step instructions in the side colomns, along with the illustrations, and you're done.

How this book works

Each task is presented with step-by-step instructions in one column and screen illustrations in the other. This arrangement lets you focus on a single task without having to turn the pages too often.

Step-by-step instructions

This book provides concise step-by-step instructions that show you how to accomplish a task. Each set of instructions includes illustrations that directly correspond to the easy-to-read steps. Eye-catching text features provide additional helpful information in bite-sized chunks to help you work more efficiently or to teach you more in-depth information. The 'For your information' and 'Did you know?' features provide tips and techniques to help you work smarter, while essential information is highlighted in 'Important' boxes that will ensure you don't miss any vital suggestions and advice. Jargon buster boxes throughout the text help you understand some of the key technical terms and more can be found in the Jargon buster section at the end of the book.

Troubleshooting guide

This book offers quick and easy ways to diagnose and solve common problems that you might encounter, using the Troubleshooting guide. The problems are grouped into categories.

Spelling

We have used UK spelling conventions throughout this book. You may therefore notice some inconsistencies between the text and the software on your computer which is likely to have been developed in the USA. We have however adopted US spelling for the words 'disk' and 'program' as these are commonly accepted throughout the world.

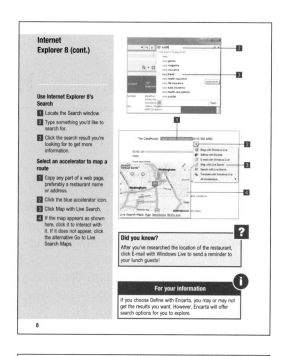

What's new in Windows 7?

Introduction

Windows 7 is the newest addition to the Microsoft family of operating systems. If you've used a computer before, chances are good you've had experience with some earlier incarnation of it. You may have used Windows 98, Windows ME, Windows XP or Windows Vista, for example, and may already know how to access the Internet, check e-mail or write a letter, all of which were tasks you could achieve in earlier Microsoft offerings. Windows 7 outdoes each of these previous operating system versions though, and offers more than a few new features that you'll wonder how you ever lived without.

If you're familiar with Microsoft's latest operating system, Windows Vista, and want to see and experience what's new with Windows 7, read this chapter and perform the exercises. If you're new to computers or haven't had much experience with them, you may want to browse this chapter, and then skip ahead to Chapter 2. Chapter 2 starts with some simple exercises to get you up to speed quickly by introducing you to the Start menu and Taskbar, and walking you through some basic tasks. You can return here when ready.

What you'll do

Use the Taskbar and jump lists

Jiggle windows to minimise them

Use Internet Explorer 8's Search

Select an accelerator to map a route

Enable web slices

Access Device Stage

Solve problems with the Action Center

Learn about homegroups

Download Windows Live

Introducing Windows 7

Windows 7 sometimes seems too good to be true. It's like Microsoft listened to you, the over 50s audience, and offered up just what you need! Do you want quick answers, automated fixes for problems, and a place to view and access all of the toys connected to your PC? You've got it. You want to touch something on the screen and interact with it? Touch technology is here. You want to be able to copy something on the screen and e-mail it in a couple of simple steps? Got it. It's getting easier and easier to use a computer, and you've picked a good time to get started.

One of the most exciting new features in Windows 7 is support for touchscreen technology. If you have a compatible computer and monitor, you'll be able to use Windows touch technology to navigate through Windows 7. This is just like the iPhone (you've seen the commercials), where you can scroll through photos and touch the screen to perform tasks, like selecting a menu or sending an e-mail.

Other features you'll like as an over-50s user is the new and improved Taskbar and Start menu, new ways to manipulate open windows, new ways to search the Internet and work with the data you find, and easily subscribe to ever-changing data like weather and traffic updates. There's the Action Center where you can get automated help for problems you encounter with hardware and software, Device Stage where you can access and manage your hardware devices like printers, USB drives and cameras, and homegroups for sharing data with other computers on your home network more easily. Of course, there's a lot more than this, but this is a good start for your needs.

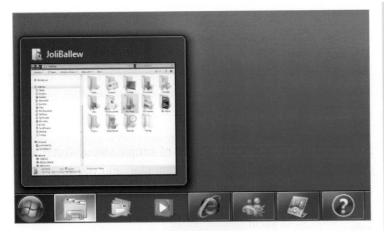

There's one glaring omission in Windows 7 though. While the latest versions of Microsoft operating systems came with an e-mail program, movie-making program and photo-management program, Windows 7 does not. You'll have to download and install those programs manually if they were not already installed by the computer manufacturer or a computer technician. You'll learn how to do that at the end of this chapter, and if you don't feel ready, skip it! When you get to Chapter 8 or so, when you start to need these programs, you'll feel confident enough to perform the required tasks. Don't worry; it's easy.

New uses for the Taskbar and Start menu, and manipulating Windows

The Windows 7 Desktop is sleek and clean, with very few icons on it by default. You can add icons and shortcuts to the Desktop to access programs, files, folders and features, or you can use the Taskbar and the Start menu. If you choose to use the Taskbar and Start menu, you'll be able to keep that 'just out of the box' feeling of a new PC a little bit longer.

Use the Taskbar and jump lists

1 Locate the Taskbar that runs across the bottom of the screen (the screen is also called the Desktop). It will look similar to what's shown here.

2 Click the Start button to open the Start menu.

Note that the programs you use most often appear in the Start menu on the left pane. What you see may look different from what is shown here.

3 Look for an arrow next to any Start menu icon. Hover the mouse over the item to see the jump list.

4 Click any item to open it.

5 Open multiple programs by clicking them in the Start menu and then note the items that appear in the Taskbar.

6 Click the icon or its thumbnail to show the window or to hide it.

4

Did you know?

When you open a program, file or folder, its associated icon appears on the Taskbar. You can click the icon on the Taskbar to minimise or maximise (hide or show) the window for that program.

New uses for the Taskbar and Start menu, and manipulating Windows (cont.)

1

Jiggle windows to minimise them

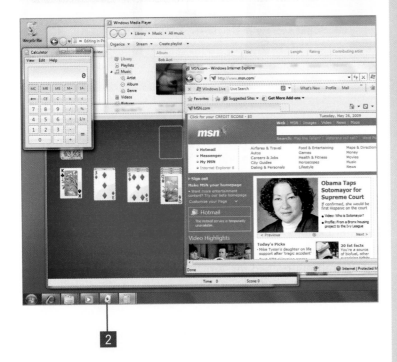

2

1 Open multiple programs as detailed earlier.

2 Click each icon on the Taskbar to 'maximise' or show all of the open windows.

3 Click the top of any window, hold down the left mouse button, and move the mouse quickly back and forth to the left and right across the mouse pad. Notice how all of the windows are minimised except the one you 'shook'.

4 Repeat this step to show all of the windows again.

For your information

Leave all of these programs and file open for the next exercise.

For your information

You can shake maximised windows to halve their size.

Did you know?

You can drag a window to the left or right to make it take up half the screen or to move it to a second monitor if one is installed.

Internet Explorer 8

Internet Explorer 8 has some really neat, new features that weren't included with earlier versions. One of those features is the Taskbar. Here, you can see the Internet Explorer icon on the Taskbar and clicking it when there are multiple tabs open offers thumbnails of each. To view one of these pages, just click it.

In case you're wondering, these are tabs that open each time you access a website. Here there are three tabs: clearcom's Profile, Facebook| Home and My Yahoo. Click the tab name to view the web page. To open a tab, click Ctrl+T on the keyboard, or click the empty tab to the right of open tabs.

Internet Explorer also offers Search, where you can type what you're looking for and select the item you want from the results list. Here I've searched for 'Amazon b' (I was about to type 'books'), and the 'live' results offer just what I need.

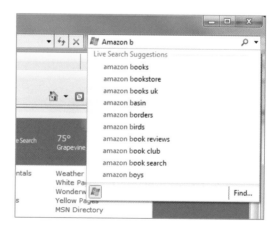

Internet Explorer 8 makes it easier than ever to perform tasks related to copying and pasting too. Copy any part of a web page, click the accelerator icon (see below and overleaf), and you can easily blog about the item, define it with Encarta, e-mail it with Windows Live, map it with Live Search, and more. Of course, you can't map a book title, and you can't define it either, but you get the idea.

Web slices are also new to Internet Explorer 8. A web slice allows you to review updated information from a website that offers slices right from your Favorites bar. When you click a web slice you've added you can see recently updated data. Sometimes this is the weather or news, but it can include other data as well.

When a website offers web slices, the icon next to the Home icon turns green. Click the arrow next to the web slices icon to see what web slices are available. Here, you can access a web slice for Live Search News.

Did you know?

Instead of typing an entire URL like *http://www.amazon.com*, type amazon and on the keyboard click Ctrl+Enter. The *http://*, the *www.* and the *.com* will be added automatically.

Internet Explorer 8 (cont.)

Use Internet Explorer 8's Search

1 Locate the Search window.

2 Type something you'd like to search for.

3 Click the search result you're looking for to get more information.

Select an accelerator to map a route

1 Copy any part of a web page, preferably a restaurant name or address.

2 Click the blue accelerator icon.

3 Click Map with Live Search.

4 If the map appears as shown here, click it to interact with it. If it does not appear, click the alternative Go to Live Search Maps.

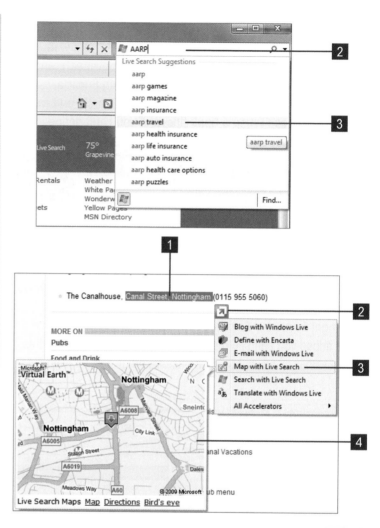

Did you know?

After you've researched the location of the restaurant, click E-mail with Windows Live to send a reminder to your lunch guests!

For your information

If you choose Define with Encarta, you may or may not get the results you want. However, Encarta will offer search options for you to explore.

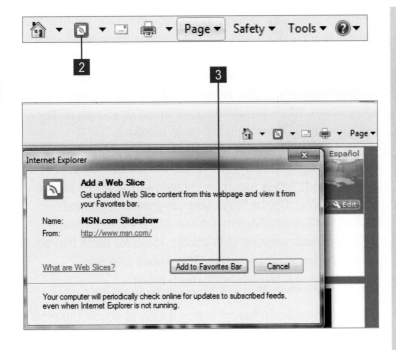

Enable web slices

1 Locate a web page that contains an available web slice. You need to see this green icon. If it's orange or grey, it does not offer a web slice. Try *http://search.live.com/news* if you can't find any on your favourite web pages.

2 Click the green icon.

3 When prompted, click Add to Favorites bar.

4 Locate the slice on the Favorites bar, and click it to view the data. Note that a web slice allows you to subscribe to a portion of a web page. Web slices can offer up-to-date information on the weather, news, traffic and other ever-changing data.

Staying safe and getting help fast

Access Device Stage

1 Click Start, and click Control Panel.

2 Click View devices and printers.

There are a few new features to help you stay safe, get help and protect your personal data and they include the Action Center, Device Stage and HomeGroups. The Action Center helps you check for and resolve problems related to Windows Backup, troubleshooting, updates, firewalls and virus protection, among other things. When something goes wrong or you get an error message, this is where you can go to resolve it.

Device Stage is a window that is customised to meet your specific needs and is based on the hardware attached to your computer. With Device Stage, you can access connected devices like cameras, external drives and portable devices. Unlike previous versions of Windows, icons for items that are not connected won't be shown. This makes selecting connected drives and hardware much easier.

The new HomeGroup feature makes it easy to connect to other Windows 7 PCs and devices on your existing network so you can share files, photos, music, printers and media throughout your home. With this set-up, you can then 'send' data to other computers seamlessly. Just right-click the media to play, click Send To:, and choose your HomeGroup device.

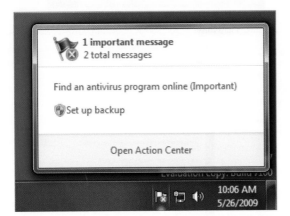

3 Note the devices, printers and faxes connected to your PC and/or network. (In this case there are 11 items in all.)

4 Double-click any device to view or change the device properties.

If there are problems with your computer, you'll see an icon in the Taskbar's Notification area. Hover the mouse over this icon to view the messages and have the option to open the Action Center. Clicking Open Action Center here is one of the many ways to navigate to it.

The Action Center looks for solutions to computer problems you've experienced either first hand or behind the scenes. For instance, in this example, there's no anti-virus software installed, which is something you probably already know about. However, there may also be problems listed you did not know about, such as a problem with a video driver, the operating system or even a mouse.

Staying safe and getting help fast (cont.)

Solve problems with the Action Center

1 Click Start.

2 In the Search dialogue box, type Action Center.

3 Click Action Center in the results list.

4 To resolve any problem, click the resolution option. To find anti-virus software you can click Find a program online, for example.

Did you know?

Because the Search information changes as you type, you can simply type 'act' and the Action Center will appear in the results list.

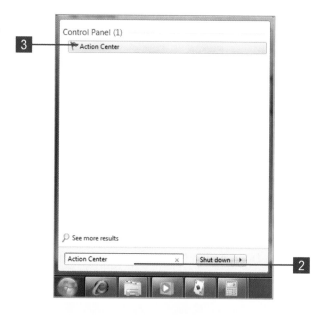

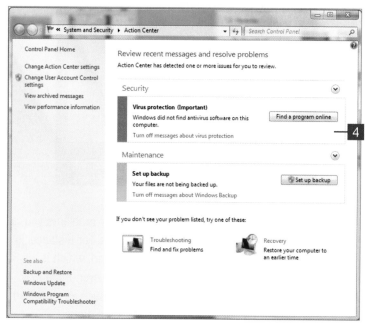

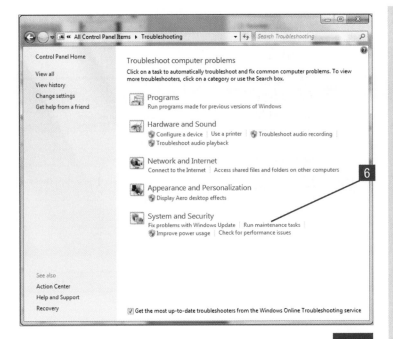

5 Click Troubleshooting to view additional fixes. Here you can access common problems and their solutions.

6 One of the items in Troubleshooting is Run maintenance tasks. Clicking this opens a window that lets you run a wizard to clean up unused files and shortcuts, and perform other maintenance tasks.

Learn about homegroups

1 Click Start and, in the Search window, type HomeGroup and then click it in the Results list.

Did you know?

As time goes by, there will be more and more automated troubleshooting options. Soon, you'll be able to click something like Fix Me, and have problems resolved automatically.

Staying safe and getting help fast (cont.)

2 If you've already set up a homegroup, you can change the settings for the homegroup as shown in Step 7. If you have not yet set up a homegroup, you'll see the screen shown here.

3 To create a homegroup, click Choose what you want to share, and view the homegroup password.

4 Select the items to share and click Next.

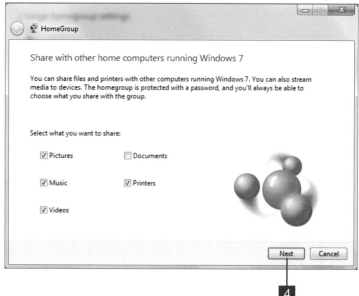

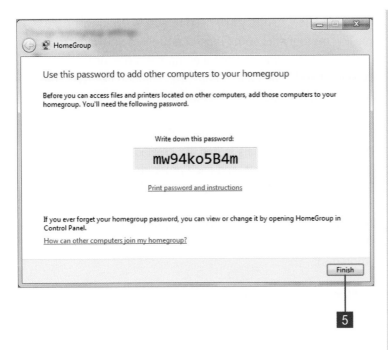

5 Write down the password and click Finish.

6 If you want to continue to configure the homegroup settings, you can do so in the final window, shown here. Click Save changes when complete.

7 Continue to configure your homegroup as desired, but remember, it's meant to be a simple way to share data, which means that the defaults are fine and you shouldn't need to spend much time here.

8 Click Save changes.

What's missing in Windows 7?

There are a few things you'll need to add to Windows 7. First, you'll want to install some type of anti-virus software. You can purchase that online or from a computer store, or you can download and install a free anti-virus solution like AVG Free. For more information see Chapter 10.

The other thing you'll want to get is Windows Live Essentials. Windows Live Essentials is free, it's created, offered and supported by Microsoft, and each program in Windows Live Essentials is compatible with and/or accessible from the others.

Windows Live Essentials includes the following programs you should obtain (note that this is not a complete list of Live programs):

- Messenger – Instant messaging software you can use to send instant messages to others who you choose as contacts. Messenger contacts are integrated with Mail contacts to make communications easy and simple.

- Mail – A web-based e-mail program you can use to send, receive and manage your e-mail. Mail integrates with Messenger and other Live Essentials programs seamlessly. See Chapter 8 for more information.

- Writer – A program that lets you share your photos and videos on blog services like Windows Live, Wordpress, Blogger, Live Journal and more. A 'blog' is a web log, and is generally used to share one's opinions, thoughts and personal information.

- Photo Gallery – A web-based photo editing and management program that lets you move pictures from your camera to your PC. With Photo Gallery you can edit, share and create panoramic photos. See Chapter 11 for more information.

- Movie Maker – This program lets you create movies from video clips taken from your digital camera or other sources, and share them with friends and family via CD, DVD or even the web.

- Toolbar – This is a toolbar that, after installation, appears in Internet Explorer. The toolbar integrates access to Mail, Messenger, Photos, Calendar and more, all from a single place.

- Family Safety – This program helps you keep your family safe from Internet sites that could harm your PC or be inappropriate for viewing. You can configure Family Safety to block websites when your grandchildren log on, allow them (or not) to speak with contacts, and even monitor where your grandchildren are going when they are online. Family Safety has to be installed on all PCs your grandchildren use though, so if you have more than one PC this is something to consider. Unless you have grandchildren to protect, I suggest you do not install this program.

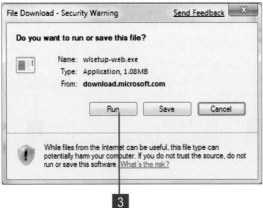

Download Windows Live

1 Open Internet Explorer and go to *http://download.live.com*

2 Click Download.

3 Click Run.

4 Wait for a few seconds and, if prompted, click Yes and/or enter Administrator credentials to continue.

What's missing in Windows 7? (cont.)

5 Select the programs to install. You may find you have one or more of the programs installed already.

6 When installation is complete, click Sign up if you do not have a Windows Live ID, and fill out the required information. Otherwise, log in.

7 Click Close.

Did you know?

A Windows Live ID is an e-mail address that ends in *.hotmail* or *.live*.

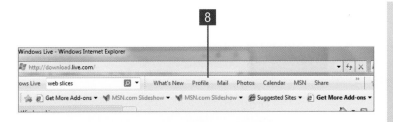

8 Note the new toolbar in Internet Explorer. You can access Mail, Photos, Calendar and more.

9 Click Start, click All Programs, and click Windows Live. Note the available programs. Click any program to open it.

Did you know? ?

Click open Windows Live Messenger to begin instant messaging with friends and family.

For your information ⓘ

Because all Windows Live programs are integrated, you only have to log in one time to access all of the programs. And because you log in, each program is tailored to meet your specific needs.

Instant Windows 7

Introduction

Windows 7 is the most important software installed on your computer. Although you probably have other software programs (like Microsoft Office or Photoshop Elements), Windows 7 is your computer's *operating system*, and thus it's what allows *you* to *operate* your computer's *system*. You will use Windows 7 to find things you have stored on your computer, connect to the Internet, send and receive e-mail and surf the web, among other things.

You don't need to be a computer guru or have years of experience to use Windows 7. Its interface is intuitive. The Start button offers a place to access just about everything you'll need, from photos to music to e-mail; the Recycle Bin holds stuff you've deleted; and the Desktop can be configured with *gadgets*, like a clock, the weather and news headlines. In this first chapter you will discover how little you need to know (and learn) to get started with Windows 7.

What you'll do

Start and activate Windows 7

Show the Getting Started window

Explore the Getting Started window

Know your Windows 7 edition

Explore the Desktop

Discover Windows 7 applications

Discover Windows 7 accessories

Shut down Windows 7

!

Important

Windows 7 comes in several editions and computer manufacturers often add their own touches. As a result, your screen may not look exactly like what you'll see in this book's screenshots (but it'll be close).

What does Windows 7 offer?

One of Windows 7's main jobs is to serve as a liaison between you and your PC. When you physically move the mouse on your desk, Windows 7 helps the PC to virtually move the cursor on the computer's Desktop. When you save a file, Windows 7 interacts with the hard drive to offer a place to save the information and remembers where it is stored. If you want to print a web page, Windows 7 communicates with the printer and sends the required information to it. And, when you want to burn a CD or DVD, Windows 7 communicates with those drives too, making sure what you want to do is completed successfully. This all occurs behind the scenes, making sure that you never have to worry about how anything works technically.

Windows 7 also offers applications to help you be more productive and do more. For instance, Windows DVD Maker helps you create DVDs (perhaps from digital video footage you've taken of your grandchildren), Windows Fax and Scan lets you, well, fax and scan, and Media Center and Media Player let you manage, organise, obtain, watch and listen to media. You also get Internet Explorer for surfing the web and the Sync Center for synching portable players for music, photos, videos and ebooks, among other applications.

There are some applications you'll need to download though, like Windows Live Essentials and perhaps a PDF reader like Adobe Reader, but these things are free. You'll certainly want to download and install Windows Live Mail, Windows Live Photo Gallery and Windows Live Messenger, and some kind of anti-virus software, which comes in both free and paid for versions.

Beyond what comes with Windows 7 and what you'll download yourself, you might have Microsoft Office, a Photoshop program or an art program You may even have applications that were installed by the computer manufacturer, like PC update software, music players, games or trials of anti-virus software.

Now that you know a little about what Windows 7 offers, it's time to do some exploring. If this is your first time starting up Windows 7, and you're on a new PC, you'll be prompted to enter some information. Specifically, you'll type your name as you'd like it to appear on your Start menu (capital letters count), activate Windows 7 and, if desired, create a 'homegroup' for sharing data.

Important

To activate Windows 7 during the initial set-up, you'll have to be connected to the Internet. If no Internet connection is available, a phone number will be provided. Activation is mandatory.

Did you know?

Clicking your name in the Start menu will open your personal folder where you store files and other data.

◀ **Starting and activating Windows 7**

2

Start and activate Windows 7

1 If applicable, open the laptop's lid.

2 Press the Start button. It's generally on the front of the PC, but is sometimes found on the top of the PC. On a laptop, it's probably located somewhere on the keyboard (to keep you from accidentally turning on the PC when the lid is closed).

3 If applicable, press the Start button on the computer monitor.

4 Work through the activation process, if applicable. You'll be prompted regarding what to do, if anything is necessary. Note that you may be prompted to click your user name and input a password, if you configured your PC that way during installation.

5 Click the Start button on the Desktop. It's in the bottom left-hand corner.

6 Locate your user name in the Start menu.

Getting started

The Getting Started window, available from the Start menu, can help you find out what's new in Windows 7, how to personalise Windows, how to add new users, and more. Often computer manufacturers add their own listings and links to help you learn about your computer and the applications they've installed on it here too, as well as links to their own Help files or website.

In the Getting Started window you can do many things, but the items you'll be most interested in now are as follows:

- Transfer files and settings from another computer – Learn about and use Windows Easy Transfer, an application included with Windows 7 that helps you transfer user accounts, files and folders, program settings, Internet settings and Favorites, and e-mail settings, contacts and messages from an older computer to your new one.

- Add new users to your computer – Learn how to secure your computer with user accounts for each person who will access it. If two people share one PC, each can have his or her own user account where documents, email, photos and other data are secure. You can also customise settings and set up parental controls here.

- Go online to find out what's new in Windows 7 – Access information regarding what's been added since Windows Vista, including but not limited to using the Action Center to keep your computer secure and maintained, taking advantage of new navigation features, using the new Windows HomeGroup to set up your home network, using Device Stage to see device status, using Internet Explorer 8, and accessing new features like Windows Touch.

- Personalize Windows – Change the picture that appears on your Desktop, change your screensaver, personalise sounds and change fonts.

- Back up your files – Open Windows Backup and back up important files once or on a schedule.

Show the Getting Started window

1 To show the Getting Started window, turn on the PC.

2 Click Start, and click Getting Started.

Explore the Getting Started window

1 There are several options in the Getting Started window; click Personalize Windows.

2 Notice the top pane changes to reflect your choice.

3 Later, you'll click Personalize Windows to modify your copy of Windows 7.

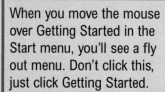

For your information

When you move the mouse over Getting Started in the Start menu, you'll see a fly out menu. Don't click this, just click Getting Started.

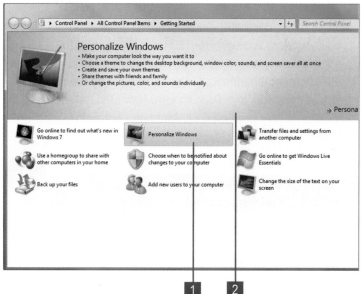

Did you know?

In the Getting Started window, you can click on any item in the window to learn more. When you've finished, click the red X in the Help window to close it.

Know your Windows 7 edition

You may or may not know what edition of Windows 7 is installed on your PC. This information is available from the System window.

Although Microsoft offers many editions to meet the needs of users worldwide, the two editions built specifically for consumers are:

■ Windows 7 Home Premium – This edition was created for the home user. It offers all of the Windows 7 features you want and need, delivers a full-function PC experience, and is a visually rich environment. This edition comes with Media Player, Media Center, Internet Explorer 8, the Action Center, Device Stage, and accessories like the Calculator, Notepad, Paint, Sync Center, and more. The key features are Aero Glass, Aero Background, Windows Touch, HomeGroup creation, Media Center, DVD playback and authoring, and premium games.

■ Windows 7 Professional – This edition was created for small businesses and for people who work at home. This edition offers business-related tools along with the applications you'll need to function in a business environment where security and productivity are critical. The key features are: Domain join, Remote Desktop host, location aware printing, EFS, Mobility Center, Presentation Mode, and Offline Folders.

For your information

Windows 7 Starter is an affordable way for emerging markets to gain access to Windows 7. Windows 7 Starter is unavailable in high-income markets like the United States, the European Union, Australia and the Netherlands though. This version of Windows 7 is designed for users with little or no computer experience and in countries where PCs have previously been unavailable or unwarranted due to price and/or lack of user experience.

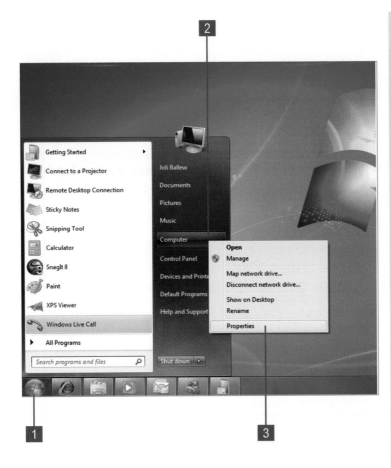

Know your Windows 7 edition

1 Click the Start button.

2 Right-click Computer.

3 Click Properties.

4 Read the system information. You'll see your Windows edition at the top of the window, information about your PC's processor, RAM and system type in the middle, and your computer name, workgroup name, and activation information at the bottom.

Did you know?

Programs that have been recently installed appear highlighted in the Start menu.

Did you know?

Right-click Computer and select Manage to open the Computer Management window where you can view system tools like Device Manager and Task Scheduler.

Know your Windows 7 edition (cont.)

Jargon buster

Processor – short for microprocessor, it's the silicon chip that contains the central processing unit (CPU) inside a computer. Generally, the terms CPU and processor are used interchangeably. A CPU does almost all of the computer's calculations and is the most important piece of hardware in a computer system.

RAM – short for random access memory, it's the hardware inside your computer that temporarily stores data that is being used by the operating system or programs. Although there are many types of RAM, all you need to know is that the more RAM you have, the faster your computer will (theoretically) run and perform.

System type – you'll either have a 32-bit operating system or a 64-bit operating system. Stating the difference would require a few pages of explanation, but suffice it to say that 64-bit computers are faster than 32-bit computers because they can process more data, more quickly.

What you see on the Desktop will vary depending on how long you've been using your computer and what manufacturer created it. If it's brand new, you may only see the Recycle Bin. If you've been using Windows 7 for a while, you may see other things, including Computer, Network, Control Panel or a folder with your name on it (for storing your personal files). You might even see icons with names of applications or Internet service providers written on them. If you've worked with gadgets, you may have those too. Here you can see a sample Desktop.

When you double-click any icon, the associated folder, file or application opens. You can add or remove icons from the Desktop if you desire. You'll learn how to do that in Chapter 5.

Here are just a few of the things you might find on the Desktop (remember, you'll learn how to add these icons and more in Chapter 5):

■ Recycle Bin – The Recycle Bin holds deleted files until you decide to empty it. The Recycle Bin serves as a safeguard, allowing you to recover items accidentally deleted or items you thought you to no longer wanted but later decide you need. Note that once you empty the Recycle Bin, the items in it are gone forever. (You can empty the Recycle Bin by right-clicking it and choosing Empty Recycle Bin.)

Exploring the
Desktop (cont.)

■ Gadgets – These are desktop components you manually select from the Desktop Gadget Gallery. The Gallery includes several gadgets you can add to the Desktop, including but not limited to a calendar, clock, currency converter, picture puzzle and up-to-the minute weather information. You'll explore the Desktop Gadget Gallery in Chapter 3.

Did you know?

You can open the Computer window from the Start menu.

■ Network – Double-clicking this icon opens the Network window, where you can view the computers on your network.

■ Computer – Double-clicking this icon opens the Computer window, shown right. You can see your hard disk drive(s) where the operating system, installed applications and personal data are stored, along with CD or DVD drives.

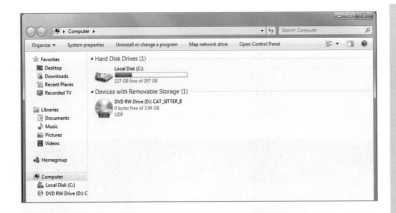

- Your personal folder – The name of this folder is the user name you created when you set up Windows 7. Every user account has a personal folder. Double-clicking the folder icon opens it, and inside are subfolders named My Documents, My Music, My Pictures, Downloads, Searches, My Videos, and more. You'll use these folders to store your personal data.

Exploring the Desktop (cont.)

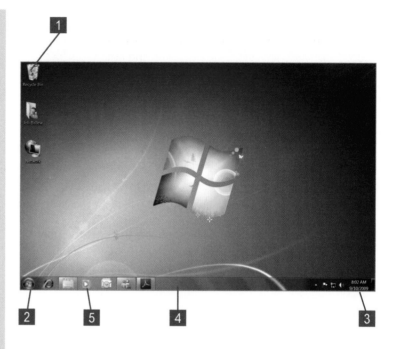

Explore the Desktop

1 Locate the Recycle Bin and note any other icons including Network or Computer, or your personal file folder (the one with your name on it).

2 Locate the Start button. It's in the bottom left-hand corner.

3 Locate the clock and volume. (You may see additional icons.)

4 Locate the Taskbar.

5 Locate application icons to the right of the Start button.

Jargon buster

Start button – you'll use the Start button to locate programs installed and data stored on your computer. Click it once to open the Start menu; right-click it to see additional options.

Taskbar – the blue bar that runs across the bottom of the screen. The Taskbar holds icons for running programs, applications you use often and icons for network, volume, and time and date.

Just about anything you want to access on your computer can be accessed through the Start menu. You can access office applications, graphics applications, games and even your personal folders. You can access Computer, Help and Support, and Control Panel too. In this section though, we'll only look at one part of the Start Menu, and that part is the All Programs menu.

Windows 7 comes with just about everything you need when it comes to applications and software. There's Internet Explorer for surfing the web, Windows DVD Maker for burning your own DVDs and Media Player for listening to music. But there's more. In this section you'll learn a little about many of the available Windows 7 features, and you can decide if they are something you want to explore and use or not. With that out of the way, you can then skip around in the book for the information you need on using and applying the feature, and ignore those you don't need or want to use.

Here are some of the more commonly used Windows 7 features, all available by clicking the Start button and then clicking All Programs:

- Internet Explorer 8 – One software option for accessing and surfing the web. Internet Explorer offers tabbed browsing, meaning you can have several web pages all open at the same time, a place to store links to your favourite pages, a pop-up blocker and the ability to zoom, change the text size, print and subscribe to RSS feeds among other things. You'll learn more about Internet Explorer in Chapter 9.

- Windows Media Center – An application that allows you to watch, record, fast forward and (after recording or pausing a TV show) rewind live TV. You can also listen to music stored on your PC, locate and watch sports programmes, view, download and/or purchase online media, burn CDs and DVDs, sync portable music devices, view and organise your personal pictures and videos, and more. To have access to all of Media Center's features though, you'll need a TV tuner, CD and DVD burner, Internet connection, large hard drive and lots of RAM. You'll learn a little about Media Center in Chapter 11.

Discovering Windows 7's All Programs menu

2

Did you know?

You don't have to click All Programs to see the list – you can simply hover your mouse over it for a second and it will appear automatically.

Important

Some features are only available in certain editions. For instance, while Internet Explorer 8 is available in every Windows 7 edition, Domain Join, a feature that enables simple and secure server networking, is not.

Discovering Windows 7's All Programs menu (cont.)

- Windows Media Player – An application that enables you to store, access, play and organise the music stored on your PC. You can also 'rip' music (that means copying music CDs you own to your PC's hard drive), burn CDs, sync portable devices and more. Media Player is covered briefly in Chapter 11.

- Windows DVD Maker – An application that lets you create DVDs easily by working through a series of steps offered by the Windows DVD Maker wizard.

- Windows Fax and Scan – An application that lets you scan and then fax documents or simply fax documents created on your PC.

- Windows Update – An application that allows you to manually or automatically obtain and install updates to your computer to keep it secure.

Important

!

The applications introduced here are not all of the applications that ship with Windows 7. There are many we did not list in the interest of time, space and importance or because the features are better introduced independently in other chapters.

Discover Windows 7 applications

2

1 Click the Start button.

2 Click All Programs.

3 If necessary, use the scroll bar to move to the top of the All Programs list.

4 Locate Internet Explorer. Do not click it or it will open.

5 Locate Windows Media Center. Do not click it or it will open.

6 Continue down the list, noting what programs and applications are available in your edition of Windows 7. The Accessories folder is located in this list, along with other folders. We'll talk about the items in the Accessories folder next.

Accessories

Windows 7 also comes with a lot of accessories. These applications are simpler than the applications introduced thus far. Two examples are the calculator and Notepad. Accessories are located in the Accessories folder, which you can access from the Start button, then the All Programs list.

The accessories in the Accessories folder include:

- Calculator – A standard calculator you can use to perform basic mathematical tasks. Click the View menu and choose from other calculator types.

- Command Prompt – Opens a command prompt that you can use to communicate with Windows 7's operating system, a task you'll probably never need to do.

- Connect to a Network Projector – Enables you to connect to a network projector when giving a presentation.

- Notepad – An application that enables you to type notes and save them. Using this application you can also print, cut, copy and paste, find and replace words, and select a font and font size.

- Paint – A program you can use to create drawings either on a blank canvas or on top of a picture. You can use the Toolbar to draw shapes, lines, curves and input text. You can use additional tools including paint brushes, pencils, airbrushes and the like, as well as choose colours for objects you draw.

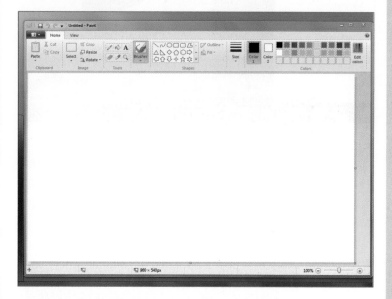

- Run – A dialogue box where you can type a command. There are many commands, one example is sfc /scannow, which will cause Windows 7 to find and fix problems within the operating system, and msconfig, which opens a dialogue box where you can control what programs load when you start Windows, among other things.

- Snipping Tool – A tool you can use to copy any part of any screen, including information from a web page, part of your Desktop or even part of a picture.

- Sound Recorder – A recording program that you can use to record your own voice (see overleaf). You can use the voice clips as reminders for tasks and you can add them to Movie Maker files or a web page, among other things.

Accessories (cont.)

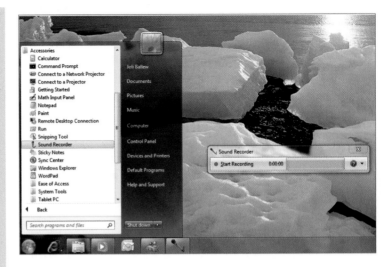

- Sync Center – An application that lets you set up partnerships between Windows 7 and external devices like portable media players, e-book readers and portable PCs or phones. After a partnership is set up, each time you connect the device to your PC, the information that has changed is synced per your instructions during set-up.

- Windows Explorer – opens an 'explorer' window where you can browse for files, programs, pictures, music, videos and more. However, it's generally easier to locate these items in their respective folders or from the Start menu.

- WordPad – A word processing program where you can create, edit, save and print files. Like Notepad, you can cut, copy and paste, find and replace words, and select a font and font size. However, you also have access to a formatting toolbar, a ruler and additional options. You can insert the date and time into a document, and an object, like a graph, chart or a compatible picture. WordPad's toolbars and interface are shown here (see right).

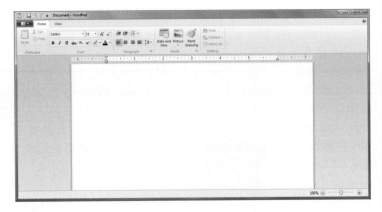

There are some other folders available inside the Accessories folder. These subfolders include:

- Ease of Access folder – Allows you to access tools that make using the computer easier for those with disabilities. Items include things like a magnifier and narrator. You'll learn more about Ease of Access tools in Chapter 6.

- System Tools – Allows you to access tools you'll need to maintain your computer's health. These include but are not limited to Disk Cleanup and Disk Defragmenter. You'll learn more about these tools in Chapter 6.

- Tablet PC – Accessories in this folder include tools related to mobile PCs like the Tablet PC input panel and Windows Journal, among other things.

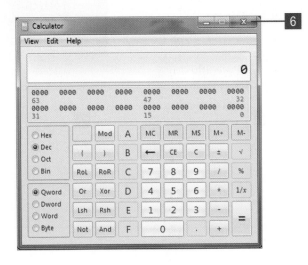

Discover Windows 7 accessories

1 Click the Start button. Click All Programs.

2 Use the scroll bar to move down the list until you see Accessories.

3 Click Accessories.

4 Click Calculator.

5 Click View to change the calculator type. Programmer is shown here.

6 Close the Calculator program by clicking the red X in the top right-hand corner.

7 Repeat steps 1–4 and click Paint. Close the Paint program by clicking the red X in the top right-hand corner.

8 Repeat steps 1–4 and click Sound Recorder. Close the program by clicking the red X in the top right-hand corner.

9 Continue as desired, exploring additional features.

Shutting down Windows

Shut down Windows 7

1 Click the Start button.

2 Click Shut down.

Important

If you do want to turn off your PC, don't just hit the power button. You need to let Windows 7 handle the shutting down process. Remember, Windows 7 is an operating system and is here to help you operate your computer system safely and properly.

By default, Windows 7 will turn off the display and put the computer to sleep after a specific amount of idle time. The amount of time that must elapse before this happens depends on the power settings that you've configured for the PC, the settings configured by the manufacturer or the operating system's settings default. (You'll learn all about power settings in Chapter 3.) It's important to note that when the computer goes to sleep, it uses very little power. Because of this, there's often no need to actually turn off the PC, unless you plan to move it, not use it for a few days or if you're extremely energy conscious.

Did you know?

You can also choose to put the computer to sleep, restart the computer, switch users, log off or lock the computer. Just click the right arrow next to the Shut down button.

The options available in the list shown here include the following:

- Switch user – If more than one user account is available on the PC, select Switch user to switch to another user. Switching users is different from logging off. When you choose to switch users, the current user's program, files, folders and open windows remain intact. When you switch back you do not need to reopen these items. Switching users has nothing to do with putting the computer to sleep or turning it off.

- Log off – Choose this option when you want to log off of your computer session. This does not shut down or put the computer to sleep, but will bring up the log-in screen. Once logged off, you'll need to log back on, usually by inputting your user name and/or password.

- Lock – Use this option to lock the computer. You'll have to input your password to unlock the PC if one is assigned. If a password is not assigned, you'll simply click your user name.

Shutting down Windows (cont.)

- Restart – Use this option to restart the PC. You should restart your PC any time you're prompted to (usually after a Windows 7 update or the installation of a program), when you know an application has stopped working, or the computer seems slow or unresponsive.

- Sleep – Use this option to put the computer to sleep. Windows 7's Sleep State uses very little energy and is a better option than turning the computer off completely, unless of course you do not plan to use the PC for a couple of days or longer.

- Shut down – Choose this option when you want to shut down the computer completely. Shutting down a computer is harder on the components than simply letting the computer sleep. However, if you do not plan to use the computer for two or more days, turning it off is the best option.

For your information

Many computers now come with a Sleep button on the outside of the PC tower or on the inside of a laptop. Clicking the Sleep button puts the computer to sleep immediately.

Windows 7 basics

3

Introduction

Now that you're a tad more familiar with the Windows 7 Desktop and its features, including the Recycle Bin, Start menu and personal folders, as well as many of Windows 7's applications, let's take a few minutes to dive deeper into Windows 7's interface. In this chapter we'll focus on the features you'll see, access and use virtually every time you turn on your computer: the Start menu, Taskbar and gadgets from the Desktop Gadget Gallery. You'll also set up your PC for long-term use by selecting and/or configuring the appropriate power plan for you and your PC, learn how to locate and open the programs installed on your computer, and learn how to use Windows 7's Search feature.

What you'll do

Use the Start menu

Configure the Start menu

Configure the Taskbar

Add and remove gadgets

Personalise sidebar gadgets

Apply or change a power setting

Find and open a program

Search with Search

Exploring the Start menu

The Start menu offers a place to easily access installed programs, Windows 7 features and applications, and your personal folders including Documents, Pictures, Music and Games.

Use the Start menu

1 Click the Start button.

2 Locate your personal folder. It's the entry at the top of the right side that has your name on it. Note that if you click a folder in the Start menu, a new window will open for the folder and the Start menu will close.

3 Locate the Games folder. If you click Games in the list, the Games window will open. You can close it, leave it open or click any game to play it.

You can open any of the items in the Start menu by clicking once on its name or icon. For instance, clicking Documents opens your personal documents folder; clicking Pictures opens your personal pictures folder; clicking Control Panel opens Control Panel. In addition, you can click a program in the All Programs list to open it, or type a word in the Start Search window to search for a specific file, folder, data item or program.

Did you know?

You can click on anything you want, open it, and then close it using the X in the top right-hand corner of the program window. And don't worry – you can't hurt anything!

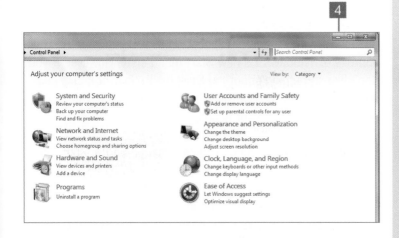

4 Locate Control Panel. If you click Control Panel, the Control Panel will open. You can close it, leave it open or minimise it to the Taskbar (click the dash in the top right-hand corner of the Control Panel window).

5 Locate the list of applications on the left side of the Start menu. These are applications you've used recently. Their position on the list is dependent on how often you use them. On a new PC, default programs and data items such as Sticky Notes, Getting Started and Windows Media Center will appear. Note that if you click a program in the Start menu, the program will open and the Start menu will close.

6 Locate the Search window. You'll learn about searching using this window later in the chapter.

Of course, you know you can click All Programs and drill into the All Programs list. In the All Programs list you'll find applications that ship with Windows 7 as well as any third-party programs you or the computer manufacturer installed.

Configuring the Start menu

You may be perfectly happy with the Start menu, including how it looks, what is accessible from it, the fact that recently opened files and programs appear on it, and you may even approve of Windows 7's new Start menu style. However, if you don't like something about the Start menu, fear not. Like just about every other part of the Windows 7 interface, you can personalise it to suit your needs.

Here are a few of the things you can change on the Start menu:

- Shut Down button – You can change what the 'power button' option offers on the Start menu. By default, the button shows Shut Down. You can change it to say Switch User, Log Off, Lock, Restart, or Sleep.

- Privacy – You can choose to show or not show recently opened files and/or programs. If others access your PC, you may want to hide these recently opened files.

- Customise – You can configure the Start menu to display the items Computer, Control Panel, Documents, Games, Music, Pictures and your personal folder as a link, a menu or not to display the item at all. (A link only displays the icon; clicking the link will open the folder in a new window. A menu displays the items in the folder as a fly-out menu, similar to what you see when you click Recent Items.)

Did you know?

You don't have to configure the Start menu. If you're happy with it the way it is, just skip this section.

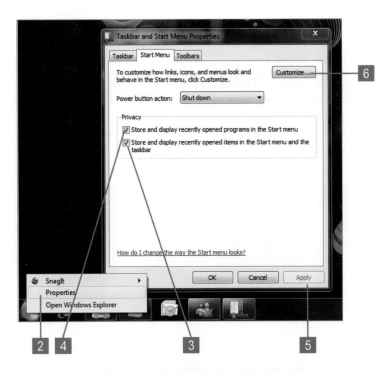

Configuring the Start menu (cont.)

Configure the Start menu

1 Right-click the Start button.

2 Click Properties. The Taskbar and Start Menu Properties dialogue box opens.

3 To hide (not show) the list of recently opened files, deselect Store and display recently opened items in the Start menu and the Taskbar.

4 To hide (not show) the list of recently opened programs, deselect Store and display recently opened programs in the Start menu.

5 Click Apply. (Apply will be greyed out as shown here if you have not made any changes.)

6 Click Customize.

7 In the Customize Start Menu dialogue box, select or deselect items as desired and click OK.

8 Click OK to close the Taskbar and Start Menu Properties dialogue box.

For your information

Network is not on the Start menu by default. Add it to have easy access to network resources.

Configuring the
Start menu
(cont.)

Did you know?

If you decide you don't like changes you've made to the Start menu, repeat these steps and in Step 7 click Use Default Settings to return to the default state.

Important

When you open a program from the Start menu, the program opens in a 'window'. When you open a document, it opens in a 'window' and, when you open a folder, it also opens in a 'window'. Note that the word *window* here is not capitalised. This *window* has nothing to do with Microsoft Windows 7 or any other 'window' term you may have heard. Window, as it's used in this context, is synonymous with an open program, file or folder.

The Taskbar is the transparent bar that runs horizontally across the bottom of your screen. It can contain the following items:

■ Icons for programs you use often – By default, icons for Internet Explorer, Windows Explorer and Windows Media Player appear on the Taskbar. You can add icons for programs you use often. These icons always appear on the Taskbar, whether they are open and in use or not.

■ Icons for open documents, pictures, spreadsheets or other data – By default, where you open a program to view, edit, listen to or manage any kind of data, an icon appears on the Taskbar for that open program. When you hover the mouse over the icon, a thumbnail will appear.

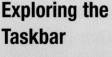

■ Icons for system notifications – By default, the Taskbar offers 'system icons' for the date and time, the network icon and the system volume. These appear on the right side of the Taskbar. Notification icons can also appear, including but not limited to the Action Center, Media Center and programs you've installed.

Note: You'll learn about using the Taskbar later in this chapter, specifically in the section Working with programs.

Exploring the
Taskbar (cont.)

You can configure the Taskbar just as you can configure the other aspects of Windows 7. There are features specific to the Taskbar that you may want to tweak:

■ Lock the Taskbar – Enabling this will keep the Taskbar in its default position, lying horizontally across the bottom of the screen. When unlocked, it is possible to drag the Taskbar to other areas of the screen and/or to change how thick the Taskbar is, as shown here. (To move or resize the Taskbar, just click an empty area of the Taskbar and drag it to another area of the Desktop.)

■ Auto-hide the Taskbar – Enabling this will cause the Taskbar to disappear when not in use. It will reappear when you move your mouse over the area of the screen where the Taskbar lies.

■ Use small icons – Enabling this will make the icons smaller.

■ Taskbar location on screen – Use this to select where the Taskbar should appear on the screen.

- Taskbar buttons – Configuring this will allow Taskbar icons to be combined when the Taskbar is full and allow you to hide labels. Combining taskbar icons will offer a less crowded Taskbar when multiple programs are open.

- Use Aero Peek to preview the Desktop – Enable this to show thumbnails (small pictures) of items shown on the Taskbar. Note that the thumbnail only shows when you hover the mouse over the item on the Taskbar.

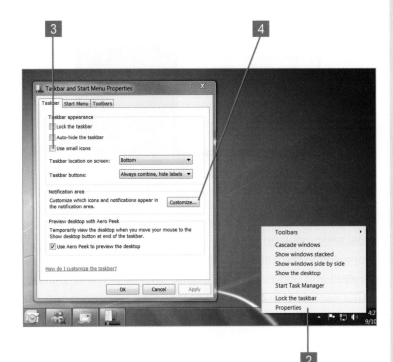

Exploring the Taskbar (cont.)

Configure the Taskbar

1. Right-click an empty area of the Taskbar in the middle section.

2. Click Properties.

3. In the Taskbar and Start Menu Properties dialogue box, select or deselect any feature by clicking its tickbox.

4. Click Customize to change what appears in the Notification area, the far right side of the Taskbar where the date and time resides.

5. In the resulting dialogue box, select or deselect items as desired.

3

Exploring gadgets

Adding gadgets to your Desktop lets you access up-to-date information on the weather, time and date, as well as giving you access to your contacts, productivity tools and favourite pictures. It's easy to add or remove gadgets using the Desktop Gadget Gallery or personalise the gadget to suit your needs. You can access gadgets from the Desktop Gadget Gallery from the All Programs menu.

It's important to understand that much of the data gadgets generate comes from the Internet. Your computer doesn't know what the weather is like outside, but when you're connected to the Internet, that information is automatically retrieved and updated on the Weather gadget, if you've added it. The same is true of feed headlines (news headlines) and stock prices. If you're not always connected to the Internet, you won't always have up-to-date information.

Did you know?

The Stocks gadget runs about 15 minutes behind real-time stock data, so don't start buying and selling based on what you see here!

You can add gadgets by dragging them from the Desktop Gadget Gallery. From the Get more gadgets online option, you can review, choose and download and install just about any gadget imaginable. Gadgets are categorised by their function, and you can search for gadgets that involve games, mail, instant messaging, music, movies, TV, news, feeds, safety, security, search tools, utilities, and more.

Add and remove gadgets

1 Click Start, click All Programs, and click Desktop Gadget Gallery.

3

Important

Make sure you read the reviews of the gadgets you want prior to downloading and installing them. Although the gadgets you'll find here are almost always harmless, you might run across one or two that don't work or cause computer problems. Don't be afraid to get gadgets online, just be careful and read the reviews before installing.

Exploring gadgets (cont.)

2 In the Desktop Gadget Gallery, drag the gadget you want to add to the Desktop and drop it there. (Repeat as desired.)

3 Click the X in the Desktop Gadget Gallery to close it.

Personalise sidebar gadgets

1 Position the mouse pointer over the clock in the sidebar. Look for the small x and the wrench to appear. Note that clicking the x will remove the gadget from the Desktop. Clicking the wrench will open the gadget's properties, if properties are available.

2 Click the arrow in the Time zone window and select your time zone from the list.

3 Click the right arrow underneath the clock to change the clock type.

4 Click OK.

For your information

Add the Clock gadget; we'll configure it in the next section.

For your information

If you have not added the Clock gadget to the Desktop, refer to the previous task to learn how to add it.

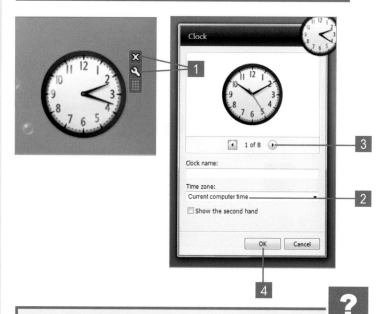

Did you know?

Most gadgets offer a wrench icon and personalisation settings. Configure the Weather gadget to show the weather for your city, choose what news feeds should appear for Feed Headlines and choose what folder of pictures should be used for Slide Show and how each should transition to the next.

A power plan contains settings that you can configure to tell Windows 7 when and if to turn off the computer monitor or display, and when or if to put the computer to sleep. The default plan, Balanced, is probably already applied. A power plan's settings go into effect only after the computer is idle for a specific amount of time. If you are happy with the current power plan, including when the computer monitor shuts down and the computer goes to sleep, you do not need to read this part of the chapter. If you'd like to tweak these settings, read on.

There are three power plans, but you can create your own if you'd like. The power plans offer options specific to your kind of computer. For instance, the power plans on a desktop PC let you configure when to turn off the display and put the computer to sleep. A desktop PC is assumed always to be plugged into a power supply. However, on a laptop PC, you can configure when to turn off the display and/or put the computer to sleep when the computer is plugged in, or, when it's using its battery.

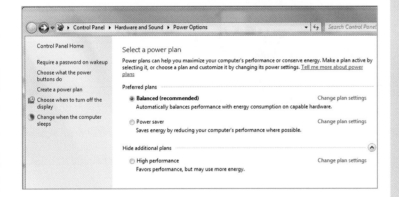

The three plans included with Windows 7, regardless of whether the PC is a desktop or laptop, are Balanced, Power saver and High performance. As an example of how a power plan is preconfigured, the Balanced power plan on a desktop PC causes the display to turn off after 10 minutes, and the computer is put to sleep after 30 minutes. On a laptop PC that is running on batteries, the times are much shorter.

Configuring power settings

For your information

You'll have to click Show additional plans to see the High performance plan as shown here.

Did you know?

It's actually better for a desktop computer if you leave it on and just let it go to sleep. Physically turning the PC on and off is hard on its internal parts.

For your information

You don't have to configure the power settings. If you're happy with it the way it is, just skip this section.

Configuring power settings (cont.)

Apply or change a power setting

1. Click Start.

2. In the Search window, type Power Options.

3. In the results, under Programs, click Power Options.

4. In the Power Options window, next to Balanced, click Change plan settings. Note the settings for turning off the display and putting the computer to sleep. Note that you may simply want to choose Power saver, or click the arrow by Show additional plans to select High performance.

5. Use the arrow keys to select the desired times.

6. Click Save changes.

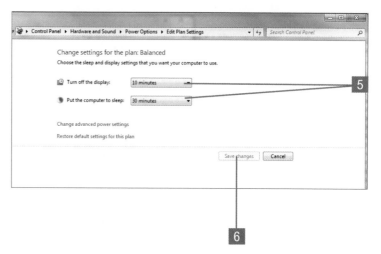

Programs (also called applications or software) offer computer users, like you, an interface to easily perform computer tasks. Windows 7 comes with several programs. There's a word processing program that enables you to write letters and print them (WordPad), a media program that lets you easily listen to, download and purchase, copy and manage music (Media Player), a program that allows you to surf the Internet (Internet Explorer), and more. You can buy additional computer programs though, either from Microsoft or any or the thousands of third-party software companies, if you find you need more than what Windows 7 offers.

You open programs that are installed on your computer from the Start menu. Sometimes, you'll find shortcuts to the programs you want right on the Desktop or on the Taskbar. You can move shortcuts to the Desktop or Taskbar manually too, if there's a program you use often and want easy access to. You'll learn about customising the Desktop, including adding shortcuts for programs, in Chapter 5.

Working with programs

For your information

You'll want to get Windows Live Essentials as soon as possible. Live Essentials includes Windows Live Mail, Windows Live Photo Gallery, Windows Live Messenger, and more. You'll learn how to do this in Chapter 6.

3

Find and open a program

1 Click Start.

2 Click All Programs.

3 Use the scroll bar to move to the top of the All Programs list (if applicable). Click Internet Explorer.

Working with programs (cont.)

4 Click the minimise button in the top right-hand corner of the Internet Explorer window to minimise it to the Taskbar.

5 Repeat Steps 1 to 4 to open and minimise the following programs: Windows DVD Maker; Windows Media Player; and Windows Update.

Did you know?

Minimised applications appear on the Taskbar. Hover your mouse over them to see a thumbnail or click once to bring the application back to the Desktop.

To use a program you must first open it. This is almost always achieved from the Start menu, although you can open a program from the Taskbar and other areas. Once a program is open, you can access its tools to perform tasks. For instance, if you open Windows Live Photo Gallery (you'll download that in Chapter 11), you can use the interface options to view photos, fix problems with photos, place photos in categories, rate them and delete them (among other things).

Note: Throughout this book you'll learn more about working with programs; for now, it's only important you know how to open and close them.

You can use the Start menu's search programs and files option to locate files, folders, pictures, music, documents, programs and even a lost e-mail – virtually anything stored on your PC. All you have to do is type in something about the data that you remember, preferably a word that isn't very common, and locate the item you want in the search results that appear in the Start menu.

Here, I've searched for 'Bocce' from the Start menu. I remember writing a document a long time ago about lawn games I'd like to try, but I couldn't remember the name of the file to look it up. I do remember the document I created had the word 'Bocce' in it, and because Bocce is an uncommon word, it makes a good search word. As you can see here, a search for Bocce results in one document, 'Lawn Games'. Indeed, that is the document I was looking for.

Of course, not all search results only offer the one, exact item you're looking for, which is why you should try to search for lost items using words that are not very common. Searching for 'Bocce' was a better choice than searching for 'games', for instance, because the results list is much longer in that scenario. While the document 'Lawn Games' is in the results list, other items appear too (see overleaf).

Search (cont.)

Search with Search

1 Click Start.

2 In the Search dialogue box, type your first name.

3 Note the results.

Did you know?

Many computers now come with a Sleep button on the outside of the PC tower or on the inside of a laptop. Clicking the Sleep button puts the computer to sleep immediately. If you're taking a break, you might want to try that now.

Computing essentials

Introduction

To get the most out of your computer you need to understand some basic computing essentials. For example, it's important to understand what a 'window' is and how to resize, move or arrange open windows on your Desktop. This is essential because each time you open a program, file, folder, picture or anything else, a new window almost always opens. You might have 10 open windows to sort through, depending on how well you multitask! Windows can also contain menus, tabs or toolbars, and you'll use all of these to access features inside the window, from importing video to printing a document. Beyond understanding windows though, you'll need to know a little about the Computer window and the Control Panel, and how to use Windows Help and Support.

What you'll do

Change the view in a window

Access a window from the Taskbar

Use Flip and Flip 3D

Shake a window

Minimise, restore and maximise windows

Move and resize windows

Work with the Control Panel

Work with Computer

Use Help and Support

Working in window frames

Many options and features are common to almost all open windows. Menus offer drop-down lists that allow you to access additional features pertinent to the open window. Here you can see the File menu available in Windows Live Photo Gallery. Notice that you can import images from a digital camera, delete selected images and view the properties for an image, among other things.

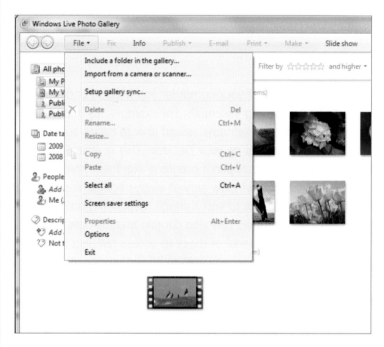

The new trend is to offer tabs instead of menus, and one notable example is the newest Microsoft Office Suite. To access the items under a tab, simply click it. Here you can see the Home tab of Microsoft Office Word 2007. From the Home tab you can change formatting, among other things. Notice the other tabs: Insert, Page Layout, References, Mailings, Review, View and Add-Ins.

Application and folder windows usually also offer some sort of toolbar too. Most windows offer multiple toolbars, which you can hide or show according to your preference. Here you can see Windows Internet Explorer, with one toolbar showing, the Menu bar. Here the Menu bar offers options for opening menu lists for the following: File, Edit, View, Favorites, Tools and Help. Click any menu title to see the menu choices. Toolbars can also offer tabs or icons, another option for accessing additional features.

Menu bar

For your information

You can explore options by clicking menu names and icons to see what happens.

Common options in Windows 7's windows

Windows 7's application windows also have their own features, including toolbars, menus, tabs and/or icons. In a Windows 7 operating system window, you might click the Burn to disc option to write data to a CD or use the View icon to change the size of the icons in the window. You can see both of these items in the Computer window, shown overleaf.

4

Working in window frames (cont.)

There are characteristics and features common to most Windows 7-related windows. This list includes a few you'll come across often:

- Organize – Use this option to perform editing tasks like cut, copy and paste, or undo, redo, select all, delete, rename or to change the layout or view properties for a selected item.

- View – Use this menu or icon to change how the items in the window look.

- Burn to disc – Use this icon to copy files you've already selected to a CD or DVD.

- Tools – Use this icon or menu to change the properties of the items in the application window. Here is the Tools menu in Internet Explorer 8.

Did you know?

When you see an arrow next to an icon, click it to access the menu. No arrow? Click the icon to open a dialogue box or apply default changes.

Change the view in a window

1. Click Start.

2. Click Games.

3. In the Games window, click the View icon to change the view. Repeat. Notice how the view changes each time you click the View icon.

For your information

Are your friends playing Hearts and you want to learn how? Let the computer teach you!

Did you know?

You can also click the arrow next to the View icon and select the view you want from the drop-down list.

Working with multiple open windows

Did you know?

Every open window gets its own piece of the Taskbar.

Important

You won't be able to use Flip 3D if your computer does not support Windows Aero or if it is not in use. There will be more on this in Chapter 5.

Did you know?

Aero is an interface feature that allows windows to appear transparent, among other things.

When you first begin working with programs, files, folders and the like, you'll probably only have a few windows open on the Desktop at one time. However, as you get more adept with the computer, you'll find that you often have more and more windows open simultaneously. For example, you may have WordPad open and be in the middle of typing a letter while you edit a picture in Windows Live Photo Gallery. Along with that, you may have Windows Live Mail open along with Internet Explorer. You may even have Notepad open where you keep a to do list. With this many windows open at the same time, it becomes important to be able to move among them quickly.

Note: Before working through this part of the chapter, open a few programs from the Start menu.

There are several ways to move among open windows:

- Click the icon that represents the window you want to access from the Taskbar.

- Use Windows Flip – Windows Flip offers a quick way to choose a window using the graphical option shown here. In this instance, Windows Aero is enabled. If you have an Ease of Access theme or the Windows Basic theme selected, the Flip window will not be transparent.

- Use Windows Flip 3D – Windows Flip 3D offers a different option for accessing open windows and is used in conjunction with the Aero interface (see right).

For your information

If it's hard for you to click the small minimise window with the mouse then try shaking the top of the windows to minimise them.

- Minimise, restore or close windows until the one you want to view appears. (To minimise a window, you must click the small arrow in the top right of the window.) When you minimise a window, it is placed on the Taskbar so that you can see the open window that was 'underneath' it.

Did you know?

If you have multiple monitors, you can drag windows from one monitor to another.

- Shake! – This is a brand new feature of Windows 7. Point to the top of any open window, hold down the left mouse key and 'shake' the windows by moving the mouse to the left and right quickly. All windows will be minimised to the Taskbar except the one you are shaking. Repeat to bring all windows to the Desktop again.

- Drag a window to the left or right side of the screen. This will dock the window to that side of the screen and will position it so that it takes up half of the screen.

4

Working with multiple open windows (cont.)

Access a window from the Taskbar

1 Locate the Taskbar.

2 Locate the icon for the window you want to bring to the front of the other open windows. (Multiple windows can be open, but one is always on top, or in front of, other windows.)

3 Items may be grouped, as shown here. If items are grouped, you will see multiple options after clicking the program's group icon.

4 Select the item to show by clicking it once.

Did you know?

You can rearrange items on the Taskbar by dragging them to a different location.

Important

There are icons on the Taskbar that are always there, and they appear on the left. There are also icons for programs that are open but are not configured to reside on the Taskbar by default.

For your information

For any open program's icon on the Taskbar, click and drag upwards to see a secondary menu. You can then opt to pin this program to the Taskbar, to make it available from the Taskbar at all times. You can also choose to close the window.

You can also minimise and maximise windows or click the
Restore button so you can resize or move the window. A
minimised window only appears on the Taskbar, and is not on
the Desktop. A maximised window is as large as it can be, and
takes up the entire screen. When the window is in *restore mode*,
you can resize or move the window as desired. You can't resize
a window that is maximised or minimised.

Working with multiple open windows (cont.)

Use Flip and Flip 3D

1 To use Flip:

   a. With multiple windows
   open, on the keyboard, hold
   down the Alt key with one
   finger (or thumb).

   b. Press and hold the Tab key.

   c. Press the Tab key again
   (making sure that the Alt
   key is still depressed).

   d. When the item you want to
   bring to the front is
   selected, let go of the Tab
   key, and then let go of the
   Alt key.

2 To use Flip 3D:

   a. With multiple windows
   open, on the keyboard, hold
   down the Windows key,
   which may have Start
   written on it with one finger
   (or thumb).

   b. Click the Tab key once,
   while keeping the Windows
   key depressed.

4

Working with multiple open windows (cont.)

c. Press the Tab key again (making sure that the Windows key is still depressed) to scroll through the open windows.

d. When the item you want to bring to the front is selected, let go of the Tab key, and then let go of the Alt key.

Shake a window

1 With multiple windows open, left-click the top of any open window.

2 While holding down the left mouse key, move the mouse quickly from left to right several times.

3 Watch while the windows are minimised to the Taskbar.

4 Repeat to maximise windows.

5 To view the Desktop, hover your mouse over the Show desktop icon to the right of the clock.

For your information

This shake feature is new to Windows 7 and won't work on a Windows XP or Vista PC.

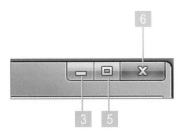 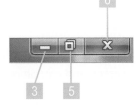

Minimise, restore and maximise windows

1 From the Taskbar, click the Internet Explorer icon. (It's OK if you aren't connected to the Internet; we're only focusing on the actual window here, not its content.)

2 You will see one of two things in the top right-hand corner of the window. Both are shown here.

3 To minimise the window (remove it from the Desktop and relegate it to the Taskbar), click the Minimise button. That's the dash or line.

4 On the Taskbar, locate the Internet Explorer icon, and click it once to bring it back onto the Desktop.

5 Click the single square in the top right-hand corner if shown. If you see overlapping squares instead, click that instead. The single square 'maximises' the window. The two overlapping squares 'restores' the window. Repeat this step.

6 If you want to close Internet Explorer, click the X in the top right-hand corner.

For your information

Remember, you can shake the top of any window to minimise the rest of the windows; and you can shake any open window to maximise any hidden ones.

Did you know?

You can hold down the Windows key on the keyboard and click D to hide (minimise) all windows and repeat to restore them.

Working with multiple open windows (cont.)

Move and resize windows

1. Open any program from the Taskbar.

2. If you see the Maximise button in the top right-hand corner, do nothing. If you see the Restore button (the two overlapping squares) in the top right-hand corner, click it. You want the Maximise button to show.

3. Position the mouse at one of the window corners, so that the mouse pointer becomes a two-headed arrow.

4. Hold down the mouse button and drag the arrow to resize the window.

5. Repeat Steps 3 and 4 to drag from the top, sides or any other corner of the window to resize it.

6. To move a window, click at the top of the window and drag.

Did you know?

When a window is in restore mode, it does not fill the screen and can be resized.

Windows 7 news

- Windows blog

- Engineering Windows 7 blog

Internet | Protected Mode: On   100%

3

Important

You can only move and resize windows if they are in 'restore' mode, meaning the Maximise button is showing in the top right-hand corner of the window.

Throughout this book you'll use the features located in Control Panel to perform such tasks as configuring and checking for Windows updates, configuring security settings, optimising appearance and adding new users. You'll also use Control Panel to add printers, uninstall programs and perform routine maintenance on your PC, among other things. For now though, you only need to know where Control Panel is and what you can use it for.

Control Panel offers access to the features, tools and windows that you'll need to configure your computer. For instance, under Network and Internet, you can choose to set up file sharing. Under User Accounts and Family Safety, you can choose to set up parental controls. Under Appearance and Personalization, you can change the Desktop background, adjust screen resolution and more. Additionally, from Ease of Access, you can optimise the display, change how your mouse works, start speech recognition software and even change how your keyboard works.

Understanding Control Panel

Work with Control Panel

1. Click Start.
2. Click Control Panel.
3. Click System and Security.

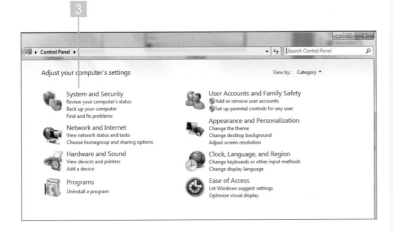

4

Understanding Control Panel (cont.)

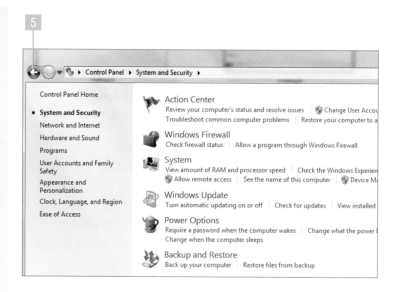

4   Note the available items in the System and Security window. Here is where you will back up your computer, check for updates, change power options, fix problems, and more.

5   Click the Back button to return to Control Panel or click Control Panel Home.

6   Repeat Steps 3 to 5 for the following:

   a. Network and Internet.

   b. Hardware and Sound.

   c. Programs.

   d. User Accounts and Family Safety.

   e. Appearance and Personalization.

   f. Clock, Language, and Region.

   g. Ease of Access.

7   Click Back or Control Panel Home, then Category and click Large icons. (To return to the previous view, click View by: Category).

8   Close Control Panel by clicking the X in the top right of the window.

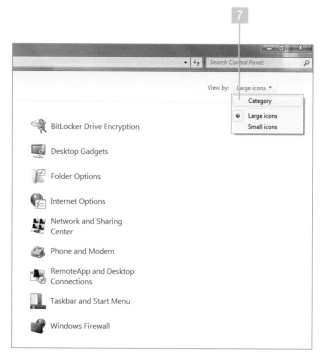

Computer is a window that you can access from the Start menu. The Computer window is shown here. The Computer window, like many of Windows 7's windows, is partitioned into panes. Clicking any option in the left pane changes the items shown in the right pane. Here, I've selected Desktop on the left, and the items on the Desktop are shown on the right.

Note: Click Documents to see the documents stored in the Documents folder.

4

Understanding
Computer (cont.)

There's also a Preview pane, where you can preview a picture, document or other compatible data item. By default, the Preview pane is not enabled. To enable the pane, click the Preview button.

Preview pane button

Work with Computer

1 Click Start.

2 Click Computer.

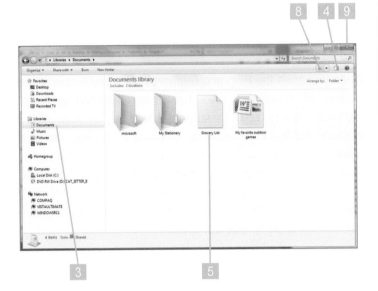

3   Under Libraries, select
Documents. Note the items in
the Computer window change
to show what's in that folder.

4   Click the Preview button to
show the Preview pane.

5   Click any document (if one
exists) one time.

6   View the contents of the
document in the Preview pane.

7   Repeat Step 3 to select
Pictures and Network. You
may have to reposition the
pane to see these items.
(Position the mouse between
the panes until you see a two-
headed arrow, then click and
drag.)

8   Click the View button to
change the icon size.

9   Click the X in the top right-
hand corner to close Control
Panel.

4

Accessing Help and Support ▶

Sometimes you need a little bit more than a book can give you. When that happens, you'll need to access Windows 7's Help and Support feature. You can access Help and Support from the Start menu.

When you open the Help and Support centre you'll have several options, all shown here. If you have time, click each option to see what it offers. You'll be surprised how much information is available. For instance, Learn about Windows Basics offers help articles on everything from using your mouse to setting up a wireless network. If you want help on something in particular, like Internet Explorer or Windows DVD Maker, type what you're looking for in the Search Help window near the top and the articles that apply to that will appear.

? Did you know?

The Help and Support window offers an Options icon, where you can print help topics and change the text size.

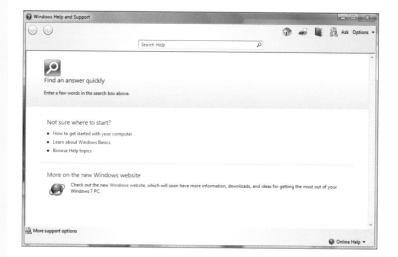

ⓘ For your information

Almost all programs offer a Help menu option. For help regarding an open program, click Help and select an option in the drop-down list.

Use Help and Support

1. Click Start.

2. Click Help and Support.

3. Click Learn about Windows Basics.

4. Use the scroll bar to browse through the topics.

5. Select any topic to read more about it.

6. Click the Back button to return to the previous screen.

7. Repeat Steps 4 to 6 as desired.

8. Click the Home icon in the Help and Support centre to return to the first page of Help and Support.

9. Click the X at top right of the Help and Support centre window to close it.

Did you know?

You can access the Help and Support centre from virtually anywhere in Windows 7. You only need to locate the round blue question mark, which you'll find in almost all windows and dialogue boxes.

Personalising Windows 7

Introduction

One of the first things many people like to do when they get a new PC or upgrade an older one is to personalise the Desktop, select a screensaver and create shortcuts to their favourite programs or folders so they are easily accessible. You may also want to select a new theme or change the screen resolution, colour or appearance. You can even personalise Windows 7 so that it suits your over-50s eyes a little more effectively or create a screensaver using photos of your family. That's what we'll do here. This isn't a must-read chapter, though; either you want to change how Windows 7 looks or you like it just the way it is. You can always come back here if you decide you want to change the theme or apply a screensaver. However, if you're ready to explore personalisation options, read on!

What you'll do

Select a theme

Change the background

Change the screensaver

Change the Windows 7 icons on the Desktop

Create Desktop shortcuts for programs, files and folders

Remove icons and shortcuts from the Desktop

Change the screen resolution

Choose a new mouse pointer

Use the Windows Classic theme

Adjust font size

Personalising the Desktop

Windows 7 includes themes you can choose from to personalise your computer. The Windows 7 theme is the one selected by default, and includes the Aero features introduced in Windows Vista. Aero offers a clean, sleek interface and Windows 7 experience. You can only use Aero if your computer hardware supports it, meaning that the hardware installed on your computer meets Aero's minimum requirements. Windows Aero offers a high-performing desktop experience that includes (among other things) the translucent effect of Aero Glass. Aero Glass offers visual reflections and soft animations too, making the interface quite 'comfortable'.

You can see Aero in action here. Note that you can see 'underneath' the title bars and windows.

You can personalise your PC by selecting a different theme. As noted, Windows 7 is the default theme, but there are others. If you have a vision problem that makes it hard to see what's on the screen try the high-contrast options.

Did you know?

You don't have to use a theme that includes Aero features. If the fancy graphics distract you or if you prefer the Windows Classic look, you can certainly turn it off by selecting a non-Aero theme.

Did you know?

You enable or disable the Aero feature by selecting a theme that does or does not offer it.

View ▶
Sort by ▶
Refresh

Paste
Paste shortcut

Graphics Properties...
Graphics Options ▶

New ▶

Screen resolution
Gadgets
Personalize

2

Select a theme

1 Right-click an empty area of the Desktop.

2 Click Personalize. Note that you may see items in this list that are not shown here or vice versa.

3 Under Aero Themes, click each theme one time. Notice how the Desktop and window colours change.

For your information

Choosing a Basic theme will disable Aero.

3

Control Panel ▶ Appearance and Personalization ▶ Personalization   ▾ ↔   Search Control ... 🔎

Control Panel Home

Change desktop icons
Change mouse pointers
Change your account picture

Change the visuals and sounds on your computer

Click a theme to change the desktop background, window color, sounds, and screen saver all at once.

Windows 7   Architecture   Characters

Landscapes   Nature   Scenes

See also
Display
Taskbar and Start Menu
Ease of Access Center

Desktop Background   Window Color   Sounds   Screen Saver
Harmony   Sky   Windows Default   None

5

Personalising the Desktop (cont.)

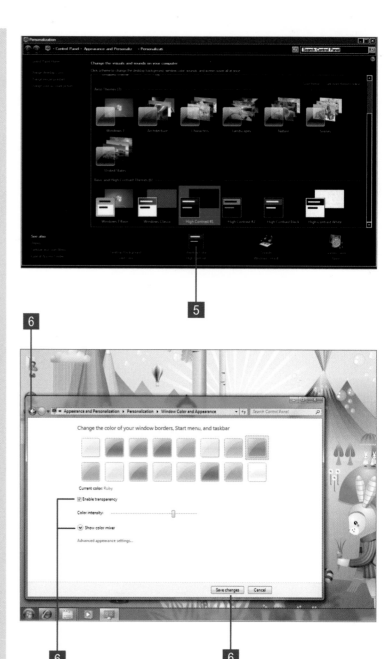

4 Under Basic and High Contrast Themes, click each theme one time. This is the High Contrast #1 theme.

5 To tweak the theme, click Window Color at the bottom of the Personalization window.

6 In the resulting Window Color and Appearance window, you can enable or disable transparency and/or click Show color mixer to have access to Hue, Saturation, and Brightness. Configure as desired and click Save changes. (Click the Back button to return to the Personalization window.)

Did you know?

You can't use Flip 3D unless an Aero-related theme is enabled. Using Flip and Flip 3D was detailed in Chapter 4, so if you missed it, return there for more information. Basically, both use a key combination Alt+Tab or Windows+Tab.

The background is the picture you see on the Desktop when no windows are on top of it. Windows 7 comes with lots of backgrounds to choose from, and you can access them from the Personalization window that you accessed earlier by right-clicking the Desktop.

There are many kinds of backgrounds including:

- Windows Desktop Backgrounds – The images are included with Windows 7 and they are categorised into various types. This is an example from the Landscapes options.

- Pictures Library – The sample pictures included with Windows 7 appear here by default. You can click Browse and navigate to pictures you've taken (of your grandchildren, for instance) and uploaded to your computer and use any of them as a background.

- Top Rated Photos – This folder contains the images in the Sample Pictures folder by default, but pictures you take and rate will also appear here.

- Solid Colors – Solid backgrounds of a single colour are the only options here.

Note: You can also position the background you select to fill the entire screen, to fit exactly, to stretch, to tile across the screen or to appear in the centre of the screen. Finally, you can select every picture available and choose to change the picture often (the settings range from 10 seconds to once a day).

5

Personalising the Desktop (cont.)

Change the background

1. Right-click an empty area of the Desktop.
2. Click Personalize.
3. Click Desktop Background.
4. For Location, select Windows Wallpapers. You can repeat these steps and the remaining ones using other options, as here, if desired.
5. Use the scroll bars to locate the wallpaper to use as your desktop background.

For your information

If you can't access all of the options in the window, click and drag from the bottom right corner of the Personalization window to resize it.

In the second screenshot below, I've browsed to a folder that contains pictures I've taken using the Pictures Library option.

Desktop Background
Slide Show

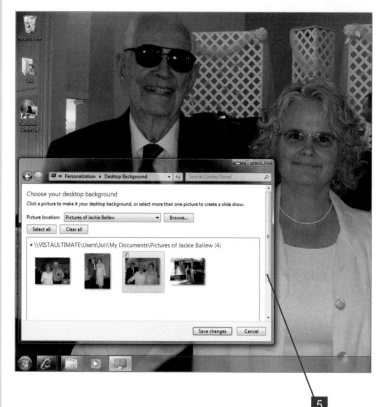

For your information

Remember, click the Back button to return to the main Personalization window if you've navigated away from it by clicking Desktop Background, Windows Color or others.

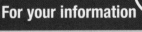

6 Select a background to use. If you want to select all of the backgrounds and rotate them on a schedule, click Select all. If you want to select only specific backgrounds, hold down the Ctrl key while selecting.

7 Select a positioning option (Fill is the best choice).

8 If you selected multiple backgrounds in Step 6, choose how often to change the picture. (Click Shuffle to randomly shuffle the order they're shown in.)

9 Click Save changes.

For your information

If you don't find what you want in the Desktop Background options, you can click Browse in any option to locate and find a file stored on your computer.

A screensaver is a picture or animation that covers your screen and appears after your computer has been idle for a specific amount of time that you set. It used to be that screensavers 'saved' your computer screen from image burn-in, but that is no longer the case. Now, screensavers are used for either visual enhancement or as a security feature. As an extra measure of security, you can configure your screensaver to require a password on waking up, which happens when you move the mouse or hit a key on the keyboard. Requiring a password means that, once the screensaver is running, no one can log onto your computer but you, by typing in your password when prompted.

For your information

If you're worried that you may leave your computer on and others might access it, apply a password-protected screensaver.

Personalising the Desktop (cont.)

Change the screensaver

1. Right-click an empty area of the Desktop.
2. Click Personalize.
3. Click Screen Saver.

Screensavers come in many flavours, and Windows 7 comes with several; the Bubbles screensaver is one of my favourites. As with enabling Aero or changing the Desktop background, you access the settings by right-clicking an empty area of the Desktop and selecting Personalize.

You can also get screensavers online and from third-party retailers. However, screensavers from these places are notorious for containing, at the very least, annoying pop-ups or purchasing ads and, at worst, malicious code and even viruses. Before you download and install a screensaver from a third party, make sure you've read the reviews and are positive it's from a worthy and reliable source. One screensaver I particularly like is called Marine Aquarium from *www.serenescreen.com*. Get the full version or you'll be prompted to buy it each time it runs.

Did you know?

Select Photos and your screensaver will be a slideshow of photos stored in your Pictures folder.

Did you know?

If you click Settings after selecting a screensaver you may be able to configure it. In the case of 3D text, you can create custom text and set the size, style, colour and rotation speed.

4 Click the arrow to see the available screensavers.

5 Select any screensaver from the list.

6 Use the arrows to change how long to wait before the screensaver is enabled.

7 If desired, click On resume, display logon screen to require a password to log back into the computer.

8 Click OK.

For your information

Click Preview to see what the screensaver will look like. Press any key on the keyboard to disable the preview.

5

Tweaking the Desktop

When Windows 7 started the first time, it may have had only one item on the Desktop, the Recycle Bin. Alternatively, it may have had 20 or more. What appears on your Desktop the first time Windows boots up depends on a number of factors.

If you installed Windows 7 yourself, and you chose not to upgrade from another version of Windows but instead to perform a 'clean' installation, you will probably only see one icon, the Recycle Bin. If you installed Windows 7 as an upgrade from another operating system version, like Windows Vista, then you'll see the Windows 7-related icons you had on your computer prior to the upgrade. These may include Documents, Pictures or even shortcuts to your favourite programs. If you purchased a new PC with Windows 7 installed, you could have icons on your Desktop for Internet service providers (ISPs) like AOL, Verizon, Time Warner or any number of others. You may also see icons for anti-virus software like McAfee or Symantec. There may also be any number of links to what's called OEM software or software that comes preinstalled on your PC that you may or may not want, including image editing applications, music players and word processing or database applications. Whatever the case, it's likely that the Desktop doesn't match your needs exactly and thus needs to be tweaked. Adding and deleting Desktop icons is a pretty common task, and will be discussed in depth.

Besides the icons that are on the Desktop by default depending on the installation configuration, there are Windows 7 icons you can add or remove. You can choose to view or hide Computer, Recycle Bin, Control Panel, Network and your personal user folder.

You can also choose to add shortcuts to programs you use often. As you learned in Chapter 3 you can add program icons to the Taskbar, but you may not know that you can also add shortcuts directly to the Desktop. Often, people add shortcuts to the Desktop for folders they create, programs they use often or network places, such as folders stored on other computers. You can even add a shortcut to a public folder or a single file or picture!

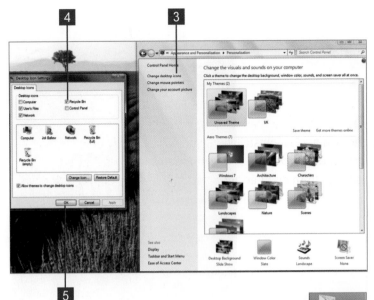

Change the Windows 7 icons on the Desktop

1 Right-click an empty area of the Desktop.

2 Click Personalize.

3 Click Change desktop icons.

4 Select the icons you want to appear on your Desktop.

5 Click OK.

A shortcut always appears with an arrow beside it (or on it, actually). Shortcuts enable you to access folders, files, programs and other items stored on your PC without the hassle of drilling into the Start menu, accessing the folder on a network or using the Search dialogue box. This means less clicking the mouse, which can be hard on your hands and fingers. In this screenshot there are several shortcuts. The first is to a program folder, the second to a text document, the third to the My Pictures folder, and the fourth to a public folder on the network.

Did you know?

If you have more than one user account on your computer, each user can configure their Desktop as they wish.

There are several ways to create a shortcut. One is to right-click an empty area of the Desktop, click New and then Shortcut. Performing these steps will result in the opening of a dialogue box where you can 'browse' to the location of the file, folder or program for which you want to create the shortcut. However, this method requires you understand a bit more than you probably currently do about how files and folders are managed and stored in Windows 7, as well as where programs files are located and what file actually starts the program. There's a better way, and that involves finding the item to create a shortcut for in the Start menu and dragging it to the Desktop or locating the item and right-clicking it.

5

Tweaking the Desktop (cont.)

Create Desktop shortcuts for programs, files and folders

1 Click Start.

2 If you see the item for which you want to create a shortcut, right-click it and drag it to the Desktop. Note that as you drag a shortcut arrow appears.

3 When prompted choose Create Shortcuts Here.

4 To add a shortcut for a program, in the Start menu, click All Programs.

5 In the All Programs list, locate the program for which to create a shortcut.

6 Right-click the program name.

7 Click Send To.

8 Click Desktop (create shortcut).

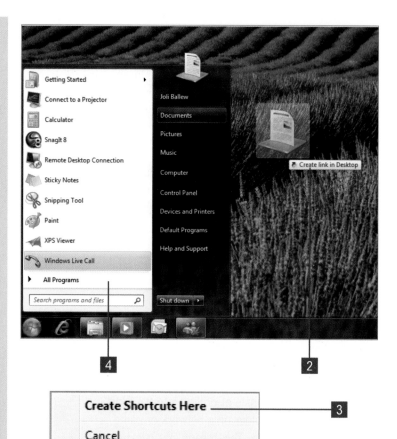

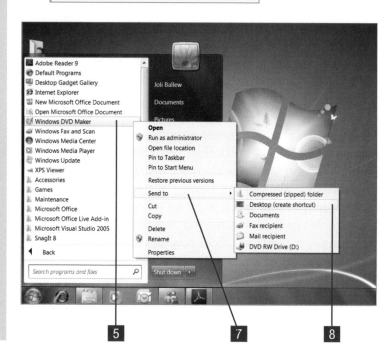

Did you know?

You can add a shortcut to the Taskbar in the same manner. Instead of Create Shortcuts Here, choose Pin to Taskbar.

When you right-click a shortcut on the Desktop, you'll see lots of choices. One is to create a shortcut, interestingly. When you click Delete, you are prompted to move the shortcut to the Recycle Bin. Since it's a shortcut, that's just fine; you can delete any shortcut without worrying about deleting actual data. You're not going to delete the Games folder or the games in it; you are simply deleting the shortcut.

5

Tweaking the Desktop (cont.)

Remove icons and shortcuts from the Desktop

1 Right-click the icon to remove.

2 Click Delete.

3 Carefully read the information in the resulting dialogue box. Click Yes to delete or No to cancel.

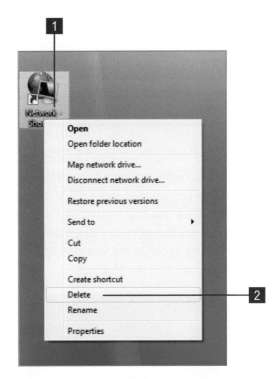

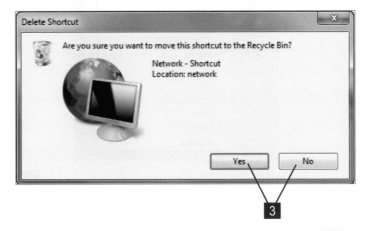

For your information

If you are deleting a shortcut, you might still see a warning that you are moving a file to the Recycle Bin, when in reality you are not. Remember, you can always delete a shortcut, even if prompted it's a file.

There are even more ways to change how Windows 7 looks. One is to change the screen resolution. While the science behind resolution is rather complex, suffice it to say that the lower the resolution, the larger your material appears on the monitor; the higher the resolution, the smaller it appears on the monitor. With a higher resolution, you can have more items on your screen; with a lower resolution, fewer. If you're having trouble viewing the icons on the screen, try lowering the screen resolution.

Here's what my screen looks like at the lowest resolution offered: 800 by 600 pixels.

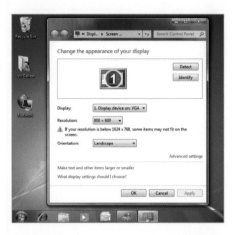

And here's what my screen looks like at its highest available resolution: 1440 by 900 pixels.

5

Configuring Desktop and monitor settings (cont.)

Change the screen resolution

1 Click Start.

2 In the Search window, type Resolution.

3 Click Adjust screen resolution.

The higher resolution settings make it much harder to see what's on the screen, and that includes what you see in dialogue boxes, windows and menus. Note how small the desktop icons are. With the lower resolution setting everything is bigger, including the icons, and what you'll see in dialogue boxes, windows and menus. For your over-50s eyes, you may be most comfortable with one of the lower resolution settings.

For your information

If you're interested, technically, choosing 800 by 600 pixels means that the Desktop is shown to you with 800 pixels across and 600 pixels down. A pixel is the smallest unit that data can be displayed on a computer. So, when you increase the resolution, you increase the number of pixels on the screen. This makes items on the screen appear smaller and allows you to have more items on the screen.

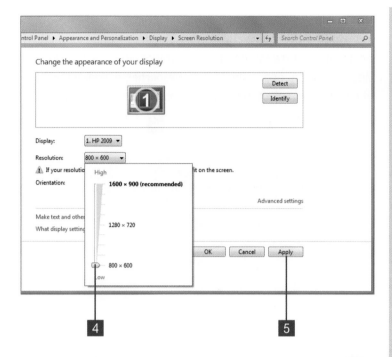

4 Click the arrow next to Resolution, and move the slider to the desired position.

5 Click Apply.

6 If prompted to keep these settings, click Yes. Note how the appearance of the screen changes.

7 Repeat these steps as desired, and select the resolution that is best for you. Note that there may be a delay in applying the new resolution as higher resolutions are selected.

For your information

If the screen goes black after selecting a new resolution, it means your video card does not support that resolution. This rarely happens, especially on new PCs.

Important

If you don't see anything and the screen goes black, don't touch anything. Your screen will return to its previous resolution in a few seconds.

5

Configuring the Desktop and monitor settings (cont.)

Choose a new mouse pointer

1 Click Start.

2 In the Search window, type Mouse.

3 From the results, click Mouse.

4 Click the Pointers tab and notice the selected Scheme. By default, it's the Windows Aero (system scheme). Click the down arrow to show additional schemes.

5 Select a different scheme.

6 Click Apply to apply the new mouse pointer. Alternatively click Cancel if you do not want to apply your changes.

You have the option of choosing a different mouse pointer. As you can probably guess, the Mouse Pointers settings are located in the now familiar Personalization window. Clicking Mouse Pointers opens the Mouse Properties dialogue box, where you can select the pointers you prefer.

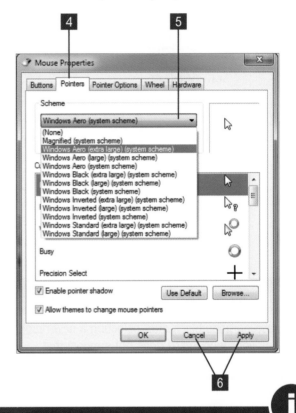

For your information

If you have trouble seeing the mouse, choose Windows Black (extra large) (system scheme) or Windows Aero (extra large) (system scheme).

If you prefer the look and feel of an older operating system and the Windows 7 interface and all of its fancy graphics don't do anything for you, you can use the Windows Classic theme. This theme looks and feels like the good old days, back in 2000 or so, when the interface was blue and white, and menu bars were grey (see right). You really can go back in time and if the last time you used a computer was before you retired, you may prefer the Classic theme.

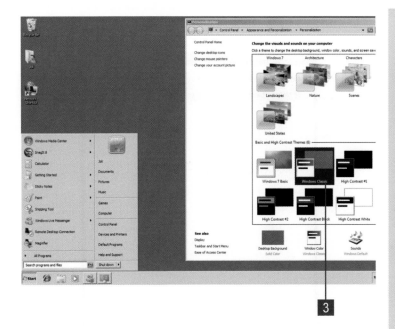

3

Configuring the Desktop and monitor settings (cont.)

Use the Windows Classic theme

1 Right-click an empty area of the Desktop.

2 Click Personalize.

3 Click the Windows Classic theme under Basic and High Contrast Themes.

For your information

As you can see, I've chosen to rotate the Desktop backgound for the screenshots in this book.

Although Windows 7 includes many features to make the computer more easily accessible for those with disabilities, including applications like Magnifier, Narrator and On-Screen Keyboard (available from the Ease of Access Center covered in Chapter 6), there is a way to simply increase the system font size if need be. If you've changed the screen resolution to 800 by 600 and still have to wear reading glasses to make out what's on the monitor, including Desktop icons, increasing the font size may just fit the bill (see next page).

5

Configuring the Desktop and monitor settings (cont.)

Adjust font size

1 Click Start.

2 In the Search window, type make text larger or smaller.

3 Click Make text and other items larger or smaller.

For your information

Most of the time, you can type what you want to do in the Search window and locate the desired link in the Start menu results.

Did you know?

The text options shown here can be accessed by opening Control Panel, Appearance and Personalization, and then, the Display folder.

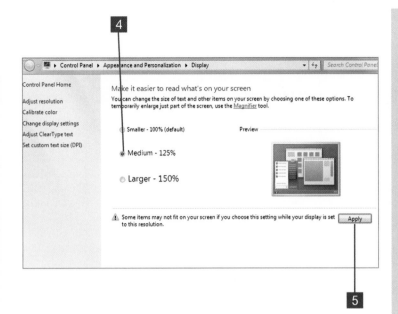

4 Select Medium – 125% or Larger 150%.

5 Click Apply.

6 If required, click Log off now to apply the settings. (You'll have to log back on after logging off.)

Jargon buster

Boot up – when a computer is powered up, it goes through a sequence of tasks before you see the Desktop. This process is called the booting up process. Computers can be rated by many factors, and one of those is how long the booting up process takes.

Browse – browsing for a file folder or program is the process of drilling down into Windows 7's folder structure to locate the desired item.

DPI – dots per inch refers to how many dots (or pixels) per inch there are on a computer monitor.

5

Using Windows 7's applications

Introduction

Windows 7 comes with a lot of applications, many of which you may already be familiar with, like WordPad and Calculator, and some of which you may not, like the Snipping Tool and the Sound Recorder. These applications, like so many others, can help you work faster and be more productive. Other applications, including Solitaire and FreeCell, found in the Games folder, can entertain you when you're not busy.

A few applications are targeted specifically at keeping your computer running properly, including Disk Cleanup and Disk Defragmenter. Both of these applications will help you keep your computer free of unwanted data, and keep the data you have optimised on the hard drive. Finally, the Ease of Access Center can help make the computer easier to use if you have problems hearing, seeing, typing or otherwise performing tasks on your computer.

What you'll do

Use WordPad

Use the Calculator

Use the Snipping Tool

Play games

Use the Sound Recorder

Use Disk Cleanup

Use Disk Defragmenter

For your information

In this chapter you'll learn just enough about each program to use it effectively, but we suggest you spend extra time experimenting with the applications you think you'll use often, perhaps accessing the Help files and viewing Help videos.

WordPad

If your word processing tasks only involve creating a quick memo, note or letter and printing it out, or putting together a weekly newsletter that you send via e-mail, there's no reason to purchase a large office suite like Microsoft Office (and learn how to use it) when WordPad will do just fine. You can't create and insert tables, end notes, footnotes, WordArt, text boxes and the like with it as you can in Microsoft Word, but you may not need to. WordPad is quite functional and easy to use, and will suit the needs of many of you quite well.

Use WordPad

1 Click Start.

2 Type WordPad.

3 Select WordPad from the Program results. A new, blank document will open.

4 Type the following: 'I am using WordPad.' (I'm using a large font to make it easier to see here.)

5 Select the text by holding down the left mouse key and dragging the cursor across the sentence.

6 Click the arrow next to the font size. Choose 72.

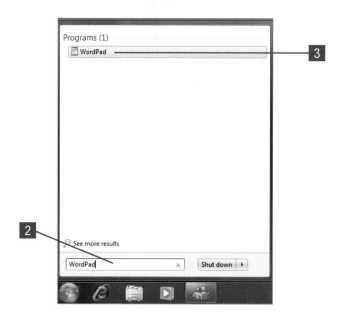

. *I am using WordPad.*

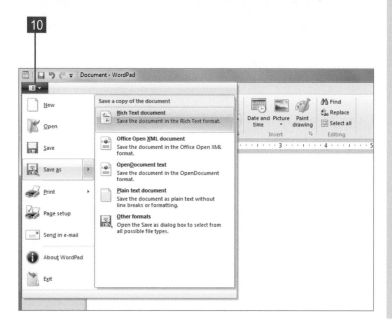

7 With the text still selected, click the slanted 'I' on the formatting toolbar. This will italicise the text.

8 Click the Bullets icon on the formatting toolbar. This will make the selected text a bullet.

9 Deselect the text by clicking at the end of the sentence. The cursor should be blinking after the word WordPad.

10 To close the program and save your work, locate the arrow for the WordPad menu.

11 Click Save As, and click Rich Text document.

For your information

For more information, click the blue help button in the top right corner.

WordPad (cont.)

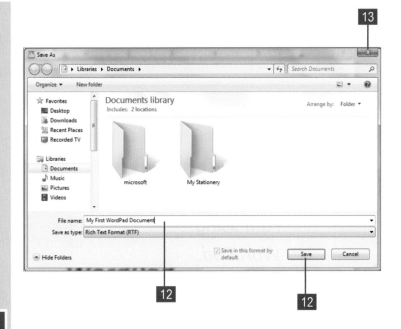

12 Note that the file will be saved in your Documents folder in Rich Text Format. Type a name for the file and click Save.

13 Click the X in the top right-handed corner to close WordPad.

Did you know? **?**

Selecting Rich Text document will preserve your formatting changes.

Important **!**

You can open the file the next time you open WordPad by clicking WordPad menu then Open. Your saved file will appear in the Documents folder. You'll learn more about browsing for files in Chapter 7.

One of the easiest applications to use is the Calculator. I'm guessing you've used a calculator before, and using the Windows 7 calculator is no different, except that you input numbers with a mouse click, keyboard or a number pad. There are four calculator options: Standard, Scientific, Programmer and Statistics.

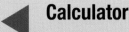

Use the Calculator

1 Click Start.

2 In the Start Search dialogue box, type Calculator.

3 In the Programs results, click Calculator.

4 Input numbers using the keypad or input numbers by clicking the on-screen calculator with the mouse.

5 Input operations using the keypad or input numbers by clicking the on-screen calculator with the mouse.

6 Click View to choose a different type of calculator.

For your information

Close Calculator by clicking the X in the top right corner of it.

The Snipping Tool

The Snipping Tool is often overlooked and doesn't get the credit it deserves. The Snipping Tool lets you capture parts of the screen with ease, then edit, save and/or e-mail your snips if desired. To use it, you drag your cursor around any area on the screen to copy and capture it. Once captured, you can save it, edit it and/or send it to an e-mail recipient. There are several ways to edit the 'clip' or 'snip' (either one will do as a name for the copied data); you can start by copying it or writing on it using a variety of tools. (These tools will become available after creating a snip.) You can write on a clip with a red, blue, black or customised pen or a highlighter, and if you mess up, you can use the eraser.

Use the Snipping Tool

1 Click Start.

2 In the Search dialogue box, type Snip.

3 Under Programs, select Snipping Tool.

4 Drag your mouse across the icons on your screen. When you let go of the mouse, the snip will appear in the Snipping Tool window. You can 'snip' an area of text, as here.

5 Click Tools, and click Highlighter. (Note that you can click Pen too.)

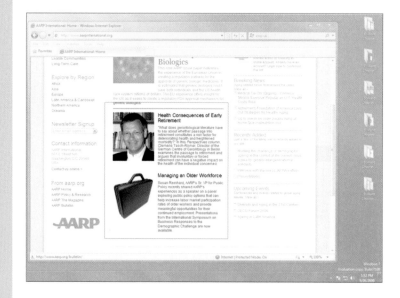

For your information

Don't like what you've drawn? Click Tools menu and choose Eraser.

6 Use this tool to highlight an area of the snip.

7 Click File, and click Send To.

8 Click E-mail Recipient. (This will insert the snip inside an e-mail. Note that you can also send the snip as an attachment.)

9 Insert the recipient's names, change the subject if desired, type a message if desired, and click Send.

For your information

Click Tools and Options to configure how the Snipping Tool should work by default.

Did you know?

You can save any snip by clicking File, and Save As.

Games

Windows 7 comes with lots of games, but we're not here to teach you how to play them; that'll be up to you. What we want to impart here is how to access the games, learn to play a game, start a game and how to save a game when duty calls, so that you can come back to it later.

You access the available games from the Games folder on the Start menu. Clicking the Games icon opens the Games window. While there are lots of games to choose from, the games you see are dependent on what edition of Windows 7 you have and whether or not the manufacturer that created your PC added its own games.

To see how well any game will perform on your computer, click the game's icon one time. Since the games included with Windows 7 don't require much computing power, chances are that the games will play just fine.

To start a game, double-click the icon. Some games will ask you a question or two before you start. Here in Chess Titans, you have to choose if you're a Beginner, Intermediate or Advanced player.

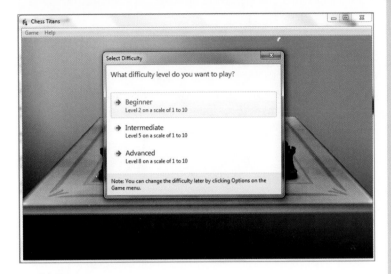

Once you've started a game, there will usually be information about playing the game on the screen, and a Help menu where you can get additional information about playing the game. For the most part, moving a player, tile or card, dealing a card, or otherwise moving around the screen in these games at least, is performed using the mouse. Third-party games require more, often a game pad, remote, keyboard or joystick. Upon exiting the game, either from the Games menu or the X in the top right-hand corner of the screen, you'll be prompted to save the game in progress (if applicable). Note that in this instance you can choose to always save an open game when exiting.

For your information

Need to learn to play a game like chess? Learn how on your own computer!

Games (cont.)

Play a game

1 Click Start.

2 Click Games.

3 Double-click a game to open it.

4 If applicable, choose a game level, read the directions for playing or click Start.

5 To get more help regarding the game, click the Help button and choose View Help.

6 Have fun playing the game!

Did you know?

When you choose a game that requires a second player, like chess, the computer will play that role and make moves after you do.

Need to record a quick note to yourself, a music clip, a sound or other audible? It's easy with Sound Recorder. Sound Recorder is a simple tool with only three options: Start Recording, Stop Recording and Resume Recording. To record, click Start Recording; to stop, click Stop Recording; to continue, click Resume Recording. You save your recording as a Windows Media Audio file, which will play by default in Windows Media Player.

You can use your saved recording in Movie Maker and other Windows 7-related programs. Additionally, you can convert Windows Media Audio files into MP3s and other file types, and play the audio clips you create on your iPod, Zune or other media player.

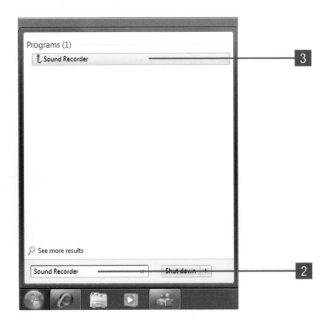

Sound Recorder

Use the Sound Recorder

1 Click Start.

2 In the Search dialogue box, type Sound Recorder.

3 Under Programs, click Sound Recorder.

4 Click Start Recording and speak into your microphone. (You can't record anything without a microphone.)

5 Click Stop Recording to complete the recording.

Sound Recorder (cont.)

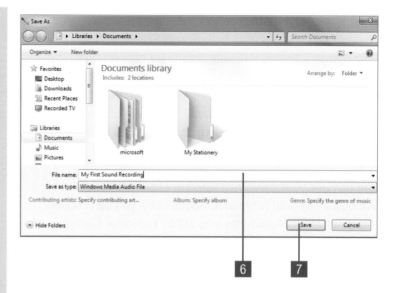

6. In the Save as dialogue box, type a name for your recording.

7. Click Save.

8. Click the X in the top right-hand corner to close it.

9. To locate your file, browse to your Documents folder. It might be on the Desktop, but you can always find it on the Start menu.

10. To play the recording in Windows Media Player, double-click it. (You can pause the playback, if desired.)

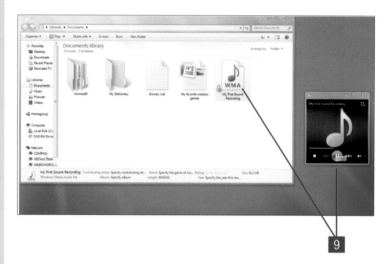

Did you know?

By default, your recording will be saved in your Documents folder. If you use the Sound Recorder a lot though, you may want to create a subfolder, named Sound Clips.

The Ease of Access Center can help you make your computer easier to use. By answering a short questionnaire, you can learn how to optimise the computer display, use the computer without a mouse or keyboard, make the keyboard easier to use, and use text or visual alternatives to sounds.

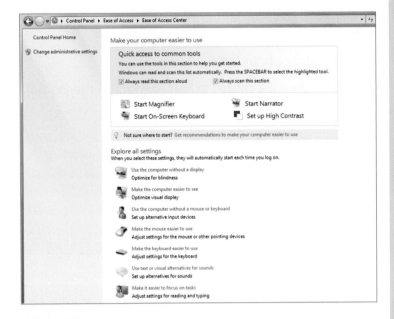

One of the options in the Ease of Access Center is Make the mouse easier to use. It's easy to select a different colour or size for your mouse. Note that you can also turn on Mouse Keys and set up mouse keys.

Another option is to Use text or visual alternatives for sounds. Here, you can turn on visual notifications of sounds that play on your computer as well as text captions for spoken dialogue.

You can also select Use the computer without a display. Here, you can turn on Narrator and Audio Description. The latter lets you hear descriptions of what's happening in the videos you watch, if it's available.

Although there are many other options, perhaps the most helpful is the option Get recommendations to make your computer easier to use. Clicking this option opens a wizard that asks questions about your current abilities (and disabilities) and helps you decide what accessibility options are best for you.

Exploring additional Ease of Access options (cont.)

Statements you can select include but are not limited to:

- I am blind.
- I have another type of vision impairment (even if glasses correct it).
- A physical condition affects the use of my arms, wrists, hands, or fingers.
- Pens and pencils are difficult to use.
- Conversations are difficult to hear (even with a hearing aid).
- I am deaf.
- I have a speech impairment.
- It is often difficult for me to concentrate.
- It is often difficult for me to remember things.
- I have a learning disability, such as dyslexia.

After filling out the questionnaire, you'll receive information regarding the settings recommended for you.

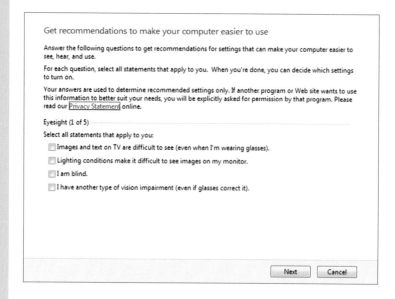

Disk Cleanup is a safe and effective way to reduce unnecessary data on your PC. With unnecessary data deleted, your PC will run faster and have more available disk space for saving files and installing programs. With Disk Cleanup you can remove temporary files, empty the Recycle Bin, remove setup log files and downloaded program files (among other things), all in a single process.

Important

You can delete all of the files listed next without causing any harm to your PC. However, read the description of each and choose wisely. If you recently deleted a lot of files, for instance, you may not want to empty the Recycle Bin right away; you may decide you need to restore something from there later. For the most part though, accepting the defaults during the Disk Cleanup process works out just fine.

Disk Cleanup lets you safely remove the following (and you get to pick and choose which ones):

- Downloaded Program Files – These are files that download automatically when you view certain web pages. They are stored temporarily in a folder on your hard disk, and accessed when and if needed.

- Temporary Internet Files – These files contain copies of web pages you've visited so that you can view the pages more quickly when visiting the page again.

- Offline Webpages – These are web pages that you've chosen to store on your computer so you can view them without being connected to the Internet. Upon connection, the data is synchronised.

- Game News Files – Information that's been downloaded from RSS feeds regarding the games you play. RSS is a method for data to be delivered to you when new information about a specific subject becomes available.

Disk Cleanup (cont.)

Use Disk Cleanup

1 Click Start.

2 In the Search dialogue box, type Disk Cleanup.

3 In the results, under Programs, click Disk Cleanup. (As always click Continue or input administrator's credentials when prompted.)

4 If prompted, choose the drive or partition to clean up. The letter of the drive that contains the operating system is almost always C:. You may also have D:/. Click OK.

5 Wait while Disk Cleanup performs the required calculations. In the Disk Cleanup Window, use the scroll bar to select or deselect the items to clean.

6 Select any item to see a description for it.

7 Click OK to start the cleaning process.

■ Game Statistic Files – This is data related to games you've played.

■ Recycle Bin – The Recycle Bin contains files you've deleted. Files are not permanently deleted until you empty the Recycle Bin.

■ Setup Log Files – Files created by Windows during set-up processes.

■ Temporary Files – Files created and stored by programs for use by the program. Most of these temporary files are deleted when you exit the program, but some do remain.

■ Thumbnails – These are small icons of your pictures, videos and documents. Thumbnails will be recreated as needed, even if you delete them here.

■ Per user archived Windows Error Reporting – Files used for error reporting and solution checking.

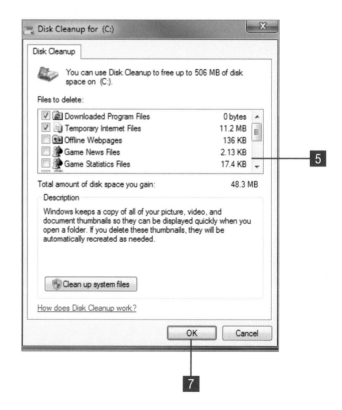

A hard drive stores the files and data on your computer. When you want to access a file, the hard drive spins, and data is accessed from the drive. When the data required for the file you need is all in one place, the data is accessed more quickly than if it is scattered across the hard drive in different areas. When data is scattered, it's fragmented.

Disk Defragmenter analyses the data stored on your hard drive and consolidates files that are not stored together. This enhances performance by making data on your hard drive work faster by making it easier to access. Disk Defragmenter runs automatically once a week, in the middle of the night.

You won't ever need to *use* Disk Defragmenter, provided a schedule is set. You'll want to verify Disk Defragmenter is set to run on a schedule though, and if not, create one. Additionally, you can change when Disk Defragmenter runs. If you do most of your computing in the middle of the night then you don't want Disk Defragmenter slowing down your PC while you're trying to work.

Did you know?

You can type Disk Defragmenter if you like, but most of the time you can type a part of the word and still get the desired search results.

Disk Defragmenter

6

Use Disk Defragmenter

1 Click Start.

2 In the Search dialogue box, type Defrag.

3 Under Programs, select Disk Defragmenter.

Disk Defragmenter (cont.)

4 Verify that Disk Defragmenter is configured to run on a schedule.

5 If you want to change when Disk Defragmenter runs or schedule it to run, click Configure Schedule.

6 Select options for Frequency, Day, Time and Disks using the drop-down lists.

7 Click OK to close the scheduling dialogue box.

8 If you want to run Disk Defragmenter now, click Defragment disk. There's generally no need to do this.

9 Click Close.

For your information

By default all volumes (or hard drive partitions) are selected, so there's no need to click Select Volumes to make changes.

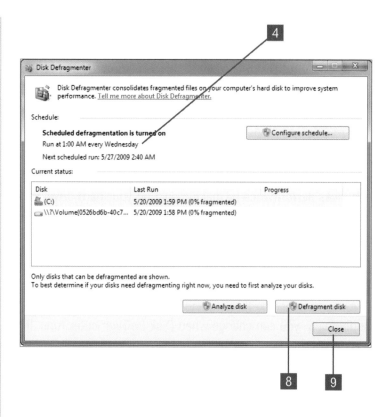

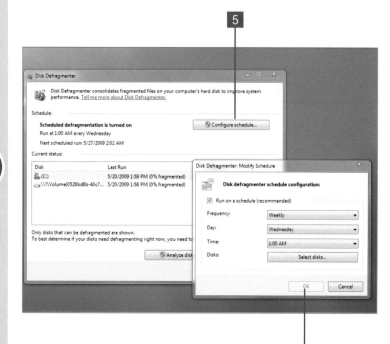

Jargon buster

Partition – a hard drive has a certain amount of space to store data, sometimes 40 GB, 80 GB, 120 GB, or more. Often, people or computer manufacturers separate this space into two or three distinct spaces, called partitions, drives or volumes. One partition may contain system files, one may contain program files, and the other may contain data.

Disk Defragmenter (cont.)

6

Did you know?

Once Disk Defragmenter is set to run on a schedule, you should never have to manually use or access it.

Managing files

Introduction

You're going to have data to save. That data may come in the form of letters you type on the computer, pictures you take using your digital camera, music you copy (rip) from your own CD collection, music and media you purchase online, address books, videos from a digital video camera, card and gift lists, and more. Each time you click the Save or Save As button under a file menu, on a tab or on a menu bar (which is what you do to save data to your PC most of the time), you'll be prompted to tell Windows 7 *where* you want to save the data. For the most part, Windows 7 will tell you where *it* thinks you should save the data during this process. This will be in a folder in your personal library. Documents go in the Documents folder, music in the Music folder, pictures in the Pictures folder, and so on. As time goes on though, you'll want to tweak this a little.

While it's ultimately best to save data using the defaults, especially as you're getting used to the PC and how it works, as time passes, you'll need to tweak the Library structure a little. You might need to add your own libraries or created folders inside of existing folders (subfolders). You might want to copy data, move data or delete it. Eventually you'll have to search for data you can't find, share data and, at some point, restore data from the Recycle Bin. Restoring is a simple process that allows you to recover data you deleted accidentally. (At least until you empty the Recycle Bin!)

What you'll do

Browse Windows 7's built-in folder structure

Create subfolders

Copy a file (or files)

Move a file (or files)

Delete a file (or files)

Move and copy with Cut, Copy and Paste

Create a search folder and save it

Reopen a search folder

Locate public folders and create a shortcut

Copy or move data to the public folders

Restore folders (and files) from the Recycle Bin

Understanding Windows 7's built-in folder structure

Microsoft understands what types of data you want to save to your computer and built Windows 7's folder structure based on that information. Look at the Start menu. You'll see your name at the top. Click your name in the Start menu to open your personal folder.

Your personal folder contains other folders and access to your Libraries, which in turn, contains data you've saved:

- Contacts – The Contacts folder contains the contact information you've added in Windows Live Mail, Windows Live Messenger, Outlook or other programs.

- Desktop – The Desktop folder contains items for data you create on your Desktop. Everything on the Desktop is listed in the window when you open the Desktop folder.

- Downloads – The Downloads folder does not contain anything by default. It does offer a place to save items you download from the Internet, like drivers and third-party programs.

- Favorites – The Favorites folder holds favourites you've added in Internet Explorer.

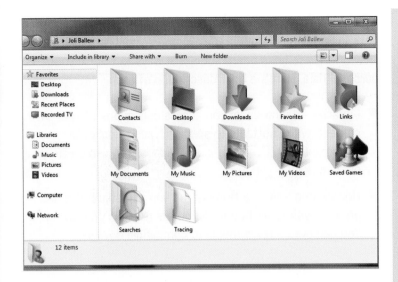

- ■ Links – The Links folder offers quick links to areas of your PC. One is Recent Places and the Recent Places shortcut (also found on the left pane in your personal folder) contains a list of recent folders and documents you've used or accessed.

- ■ My Documents – The My Documents folder contains documents you've saved, subfolders you've created, subfolders programs have created and folders created by Windows 7 including My Stationery.

- ■ My Music – The Music library contains music you save to the PC.

- ■ Pictures – The My Pictures folder contains pictures you save to the PC.

- ■ My Videos – The My Video folder contains videos you save to the PC.

- ■ Saved Games – The Saved Games folder holds games you save.

- ■ Searches – The Searches folder holds searches you create and save.

- ■ Tracing – Holds system information you don't need to worry about.

Understanding Windows 7's built-in folder structure (cont.)

On the left side of your personal folder window are several links including links to Libraries, Homegroup, Computer and Network. These links offers additional ways to access your personal data. Here's a brief description of each:

- Libraries – Libraries let you access collections of your own content, with shortcuts to specific types of data like documents, music, pictures and videos. You can create your own libraries if you like.

- Homegroup – With a Homegroup you can share files and printers with other home computers running Windows 7. You can even stream media to compatible devices.

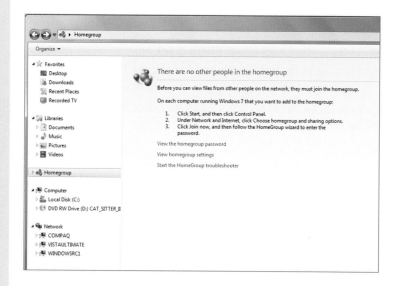

- Computer – The Computer icon lets you view the hard drives on your computer, including any external or detachable drives.

? Did you know?

When you plug in an external drive, like a flash drive, a new letter will appear in the Computer window. When you unplug it, the letter disappears.

- Network – The Network icon lets you view (and access, with proper credentials) other computers on your network.

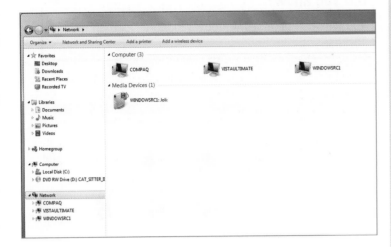

For your information

Right-click under the Network icon and click Show All Folders to see every available folder in the list. Repeat to hide them.

When you're ready to save data, you're going to want to save it to the folder that most closely matches to data you're saving. Documents should go in the Documents folder, pictures in the Pictures folder, etc. Note that when you save a picture to the Pictures folder, you'll also be able to access that picture from the Pictures Library. The same is true of documents, videos and music.

Understanding Windows 7's built-in folder structure (cont.)

Browse Windows 7's built-in folder structure

1. Click Start.

2. Click the icon with your name on it. This will open your personal folder.

3. Drag the divider bars so that you can see the panes completely.

4. Under Favorites, click Desktop. You can see everything currently on your Desktop.

5. Continue experimenting until you are comfortable with the layout.

6. Click the red X at the top right of the window to close it.

Did you know?

You can also click the Windows Explorer icon on the Taskbar.

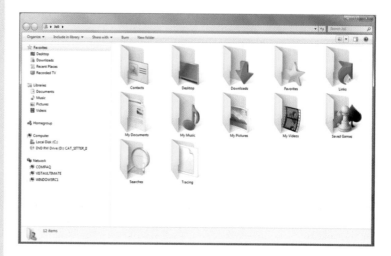

Did you know?

Libraries contain links to data you define, like music or video. Libraries allow you to access specific data types quickly and without searching lots of other folders.

While Windows 7's default folders will suit your needs for a while, it won't last. Soon you'll need to create subfolders inside those folders to manage your data and keep it organised. For instance, inside the Documents folder, you may need to create a subfolder called Tax Information to hold scanned receipts, tax records and account information. Inside the Pictures folder you might create folders named 2009, 2010, 2011, or Weddings, Holidays, Family, and so on.

The idea behind extending Windows 7's folder structure is to personalise it to meet your needs. If you travel a lot, you might want to create an entirely new folder called Travel, and put folders and subfolders in that named according to the cities or countries you visit. And, you could keep everything related to that city or country in it, including maps, documents, pictures and videos, and ignore all of Windows 7's existing folders altogether. Other folders you might consider creating include:

- Graduations.
- Genealogy.
- Places to Visit.
- Quilting Patterns.
- Bike Trails.
- Campsites.
- Letters to Family.
- Pets.
- Doctor and Hospital Information.
- Recipes.
- Home Improvements.
- Scanned Receipts.

Creating your own folders

Did you know?

You can create a new folder just about anywhere; on the Desktop, in an existing folder or in a folder you create yourself. If you have an external hard drive or networked computer, you can create a folder called Backup in any of the Public folders and store backup data there.

7

Creating your own folders (cont.)

Create subfolders

1. Open any folder you'd like to create a subfolder for.

2. Right-click inside the folder.

3. Click New, and click Folder.

4. Type a name for the folder and press Enter on the keyboard.

Now, before we get started, consider this. Your personal folder, the one with your name on it that you can access from the Start menu, holds Windows 7's default *libraries* like Documents, Music, Videos and Pictures. It's those libraries that hold your *folders*, like My Documents, My Music, My Videos and My Pictures. If you're going to create new folders and subfolders, this is the place to create them. This will make them easy to find, but will also make them easy to back up. When you use Windows 7's Backup and Restore program, it'll automatically back up everything there. If you have folders scattered about the hard drive, you'll have to manually tell the program where they are and that you want to back them up. That said, in the following steps, you'll create folders and subfolders in your personal folder, noting that you can create folders anywhere else on the hard drive, even the Desktop.

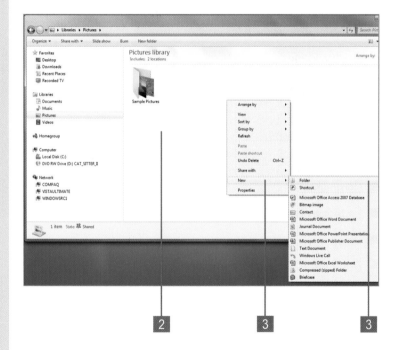

Did you know?

You can also create new libraries, but we think that creating folders and subfolders will suffice for quite some time.

For your information

When a folder or subfolder is empty, its icon indicates this. When data is added to the folder, this is noted in the icon image.

For your information

To create a second folder inside a folder, right-click an empty area inside the folder and repeat these steps.

Did you know?

When you right-click inside a folder, you will see more than New (see Step 3). One thing you will see is Sort by. The default sorting option is Ascending, but you can sort data in other ways too, including Name, Date Modified, Type, Size, and more. Feel free to experiment with these settings. You can't hurt anything!

Copying, moving and deleting files

It might be helpful to think of folders in a more physical way. For instance, you could allot an entire physical file cabinet drawer to documents, name the drawer Documents and then create subfolders to organise, sort and manage the printed documents you have. You can do the same thing on your computer, except on a computer the data is all digital, not physical. Thus, the next logical step after creating folders and subfolders is to put data in those folders. This will help you keep the data organised and easily available, just as you would in a filing cabinet.

You may want to start with your pictures. Often, the Windows 7 Pictures folder becomes filled with unorganised pictures from your digital camera, the web, e-mails or other sources. (In my case it becomes unorganised due to screenshots for books!) To organise the data inside the folder, you create subfolders inside the Pictures folder and then move pictures into them to arrange and manage them. That's what we'll do in the next exercise.

Before we start moving data around though, it's important to understand the difference between copying and moving. When you copy something, an exact duplicate is made. The original copy of the data remains where it is, and a copy of it is placed somewhere else. For the most part, this is not what you want to do when organising data. When organising data, you want to move the data. If a picture of a graduation needs to be put in the Graduation Pictures folder, you need to move it, not copy it.

When you back up data you want to copy it. This is about the only time you will want to copy data. And, you'll want to copy the data to a source you'll keep away from your PC. You can copy data to a CD or DVD drive, to an external hard drive or to a network drive. Copying allows you to create a back-up of the data in one place, like a friend's house or a safety deposit box, while keeping a local copy available for immediate use.

To move and copy data, you have quite a few choices. The first is to drag and drop with the mouse. You can either left-click and drag and drop the data using a mouse, or you can right-click and drag and drop the data with the mouse. Left-clicking is easier, but there are rules to remember. When you right-click, there are no rules to remember. Let's look at the rules first, and then I'll suggest you always right-click when you drag and drop data.

When you drag and drop data using a left-click, certain things happen by default. If you drag and drop data from a folder to the Desktop, the file is always moved. That means the file (or data or picture) is no longer in the folder, it's now on the Desktop. If you drag and drop from one folder to another, again, the file is moved out of the original folder and into the new one. If you drag and drop from one folder on one hard drive to a folder on another, the data is copied. Windows 7 assumes in this case that you are backing up data to a secondary source and don't want to move it. There are more rules, but let's cut our losses. If you right-click and drag and drop data, *you* get to choose what to do with the data. You can copy, move, create a shortcut or even cancel.

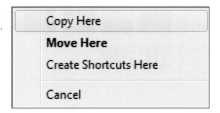

Copying, moving and deleting files (cont.)

Copy a file (or files)

1 Click Start.

2 Click Pictures.

3 Take a look at the data inside your Pictures library. You may see pictures that are unorganised, not in subfolders or, perhaps, not even pictures at all. If you only see the Sample Pictures folder, open it.

4 Right-click any picture, either from the Sample Pictures folder or any of your personal pictures.

5 Drag and drop the image to the Desktop. (Don't worry that it says Move to Desktop, since you right-clicked, you get to decide if it's moved or copied.)

6 Let go of the mouse, and select Copy Here.

7 Notice the picture now appears on the Desktop and also in the folder. It's been copied.

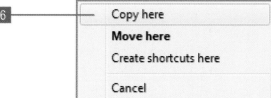

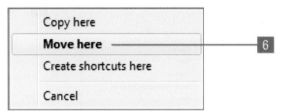

Copy here

Move here ——————————— 6

Create shortcuts here

Cancel

Move a file (or files)

1 (The Pictures folder may already be open and sized properly. If so, skip to Step 5.) Click Start.

2 Click Pictures.

3 Take a look at the data inside your Pictures library. You may see pictures that are unorganised, not in subfolders or, perhaps, not even pictures at all. If you only see the Sample Pictures folder, open it.

4 Right-click any picture, either from the Sample Pictures folder or any of your personal pictures.

5 Drag and drop the image to the Desktop. (Don't worry that it says Move to Desktop, since you right-clicked, you get to decide if it's moved or copied.)

6 Let go of the mouse, and select Move Here.

7 Notice the picture now appears on the Desktop but is not longer in the folder. It's been moved.

Copying, moving and deleting files (cont.)

Delete a file (or files)

1. Right-click any file or folder you want to delete.
2. Click Delete.

Deleting files and folders is as simple as right-clicking and selecting Delete. When you delete an item, library or a folder the deleted data goes to the Recycle Bin. If you delete something by mistake, you can get it back if need be, by opening the Recycle Bin, locating the data, and clicking Restore. Note that once you empty the Recycle Bin, that data is no longer available for restoring.

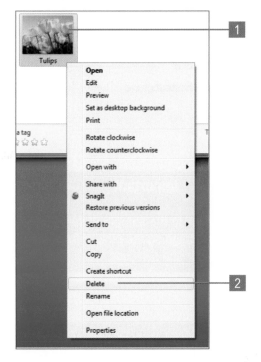

As noted, you can also move and copy data using the commands Cut, Copy and Paste. You access these commands from the window's Organize menu or by right-clicking.

- Cut – Copies the data to Windows 7's Clipboard (a virtual, temporary, holding area). The data will be deleted from its original location as soon as you 'paste' it somewhere else. Pasting Cut data moves the data.

- Copy – Copies the data to Windows 7's Clipboard (a virtual, temporary, holding area). The data will not be deleted from its original location even when you 'paste' it somewhere else. Pasting copied data will copy the data, not move it.

- Paste – Copies or moves the data to the new location. If the data was cut, it will be moved. If the data was copied, it will be copied.

Move and copy with Cut, Copy and Paste

7

1. Right-click any data you want to move or copy.

2. To move the data, click Cut. To copy the data, click Copy.

3. Browse to the location to copy or move the file to. This may require you click Start, and select your personal library, and then double-click a library, folder and/or subfolder inside it.

4. Right-click and select Paste.

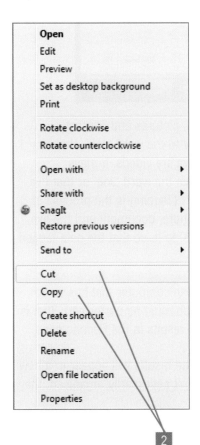

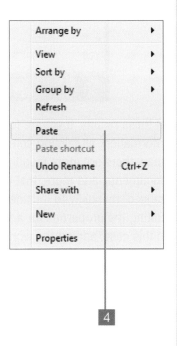

Using Search and saving the results

Windows 7 lets you search from the Search menu, as you know. Just click Start and, in the Search dialogue box, type a few letters of what you're looking for, and results will appear in a list. Here, I've typed 'Joli', and the results are shown.

In these results, there are folders, pictures and contact information, all relating somehow to the word 'Joli'. However, I know there are more results. There are videos, e-mails, documents, and more, that contain the word 'Joli' or that I've 'tagged' manually to include 'Joli'. (Tagging is the process of editing the properties for a file, photo, document and the like; in this case, adding the word 'Joli' to it, so that the data tagged appears in search results.)

In order to locate everything on the computer that has to do with 'Joli', a more thorough search must be performed. That is easily done by clicking See more results in the Results pane.

After clicking See more results, the results will appear in a new window. Although the results aren't necessarily organised, they do appear (see right).

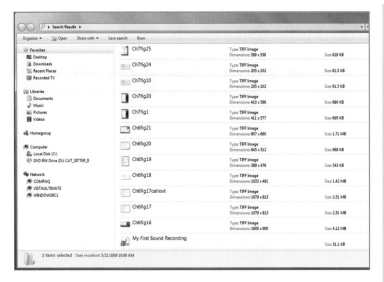

Organise search results

If you're looking for something in particular, you'll probably want to organise the results in a way that promotes actually finding what you want. You can do that by switching the view to Details. Then, you can sort and filter the data by Name, Date modified, Type, Folder and Size by clicking the arrow next to that word on the appropriate column. This is a Details view.

The most-used columns include:

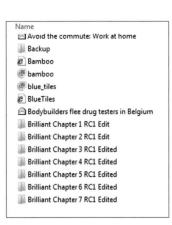

- Name – Click Name to organise the data by the data's name. If you know the name of the file, picture or folder you want, this is a good option. You can filter this by only including certain groups of alpha fields, like A–H.

■ Date modified – Click Date modified to organise the data by date. If you know the approximate date of the last modification to the file, this is a good option. You can filter these results by only including certain dates, like Earlier this year, Earlier this month, and more. You can even select a specific date using a calendar.

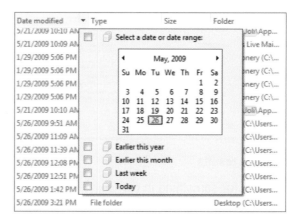

■ Type – Click Type to organise the data by the type of data it is, such as an image, document, shortcut, document, etc. This is a good option if you know you're looking for a photo, document and the like. You can filter the results down to one type of data, such as JPEG Image.

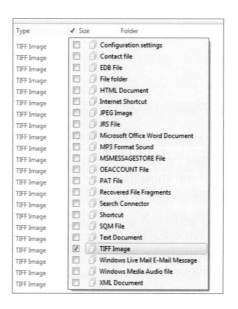

There are other filtering options, including Folder and Size, and you can add your own column headings. Just right-click on any column head (like Name or Date modified) to see the resulting drop-down list and change the columns that appear. Select or deselect these or click More... to access additional options.

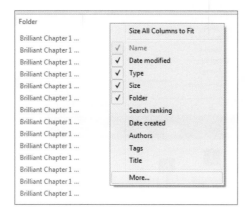

Creating a search folder

Once you perform a search, and the search results appear in a window, and even after sorting through and filtering the results, you can save the results in a search folder. Once saved, you can access the results any time you like, simply by opening the folder. Search folders are 'smart' too; each time you open the folder after saving it, it performs a new search and adds any new data it finds that matches the search folder's criteria. There are all sorts of uses for search folders, so let your imagination run wild. You can create a search folder for anything you can type into the Search dialogue box.

Did you know?

A search folder only offers a place to access data that matches the search criteria; it does not move the data there or create copies of it.

For your information

To show the dialogue box in this screenshot, right-click next to any column name, like Folder or Size.

Using Search and saving the results (cont.)

Create a search folder and save it

1. Click Start.

2. In the Search dialogue box, type something you'd like to search for. For practice, you should type in your own first name.

3. Click See more results.

4. Click the View icon and select Details.

5. Filter and sort the data as desired using the methods described earlier. Here, I've selected all of the TIFF images.

6. Click Save search.

7. Name the search descriptively.

8. Click Save.

9. Close the window by clicking the X in the top right-hand corner.

! Important

The search folder will be stored in your library under Favorites. You'll learn how to open that folder and the saved search folders next.

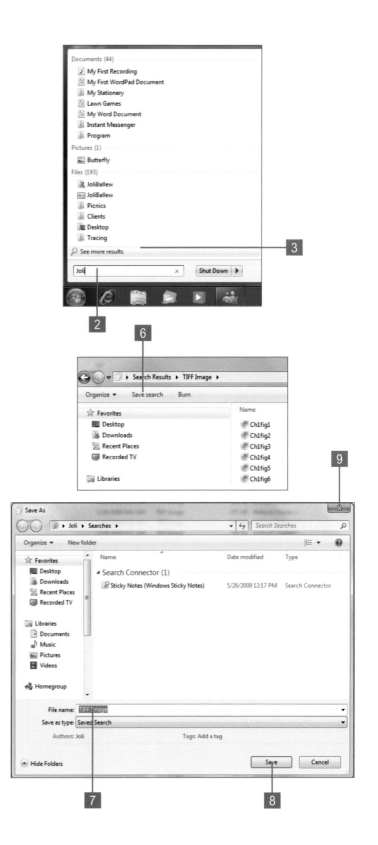

Reopening a search folder

Once a search folder is saved, you can access it and its contents just like any other folder on your hard drive. By default, search folders are saved in your personal library, under Favorites.

Every time you access the folder, a new search is performed, to make sure the folder's contents are up to date. That means if you add data to the PC that matches the criteria for the search folder, the next time you open the folder, that data will be included.

You may see results in a folder that do not seem to belong. That's because an item always gets tagged with information as it's copied or saved to the PC. That tag will include the date it was put on the PC, the owner of the data or even what type of camera was used to obtain the picture. So, although you may not be in a picture that appears in a folder from results obtained by searching for your own name, the picture may be in that folder because you are the 'author' or 'owner' of that picture, i.e. because you put it on the computer. So don't be surprised if search folders contain odd-looking data; it's normal.

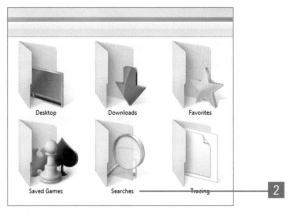

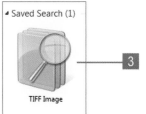

Reopen a search folder

1. Click Start, and click your personal folder.
2. Locate the Searches folder under Favorites.
3. Click to open it and see your saved searches.

For your information

Your personal folder is the folder with your name on it.

Using public folders

You can share your personal data with Windows 7's built-in public folders. There are other ways to share, but public folders are extremely easy to use and require no knowledge of permissions, user accounts or network sharing rules. With public folders, you simply move, copy or save the data you want to share in the appropriate public folder, and anyone with an account on the computer can access it. You can also configure the public folder to share files with people using other computers on your local network. The nice part is, there's very little configuration involved.

Public folders are a great way to keep multiple-user PCs organised, and to avoid multiple copies of data. Instead of having two copies of your last holiday, one copy under your account and the other under your partner's account, you can have one copy and store it in the Public Pictures folder. There, you can both access the pictures and don't have to have two copies of it stored. The same is true of videos. You can even create your own public subfolder for e-mail attachments. Save funny attachments there instead of e-mailing them to your partner (who uses the same PC) and you'll reduce the clutter created by having two copies of the e-mail and attachment on the PC.

If you don't want everyone who has access to the computer to be able to view shared data, you'll have to choose another option for sharing data. There are several including manually sharing your personal folders and setting the required permissions, sharing on CDs and DVDs, sharing via e-mail, and even sharing using instant messaging programs such as Windows Live Messenger. However, public folders are the easiest to use and manage, and the easiest to keep organised.

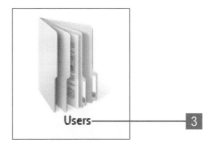

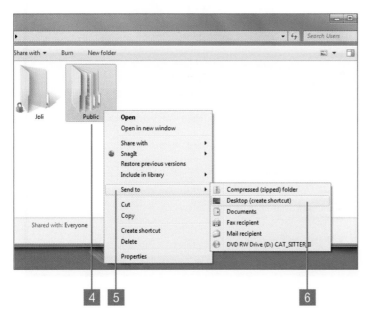

Locate public folders and create a shortcut

7

1 Click Start and click Computer.

2 Double-click Local Disk (C:).

3 Double-click Users.

4 To create a shortcut on the Desktop for the public folder, which is a good idea if you plan to use it often, right-click Public.

5 Click Send to.

6 Click Desktop (create shortcut).

Using public folders (cont.)

8

7 Double-click Public (or the new Public shortcut) to see the contents of the public folder:

   a. Public Documents;

   b. Public Downloads;

   c. Public Music;

   d. Public Pictures;

   e. Public Recorded TV;

   f. Public Videos.

8 Click the red X in the top right-hand corner of the Public window to close it.

Copy or move data to the public folders

1 Open the public folder using its shortcut.

2 Drag the Public window all the way off the right side of the screen. It will reposition itself automatically on the right side of the Desktop.

?

Did you know?

If you want to move the shortcut to a new location, such as your personal folder, just drag and drop it there.

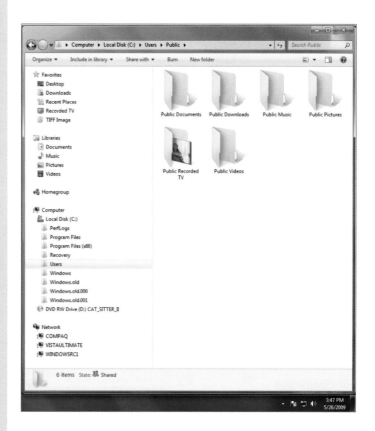

You can save any file to any public folder by browsing to it using the application's Save as dialogue box. Here is WordPad's Save As dialogue box. Here, under Favorites, I've selected Desktop, because the shortcut I created to the public folders is on the Desktop. I can then open the Public library and choose Public Documents to save the file so that it is shared with others.

In this screenshot, in WordPad's Save As dialogue box, we clicked Desktop, and then clicked the shortcut to Public. Finally, we chose the Public Documents folder. Notice the *path* name in the address bar.

Because virtually all programs offer a Save as dialogue box, it's possible to save all of your data in public folders, if you desire. To do so, when saving, simply choose to save to one of the Public folders instead of your personal folders.

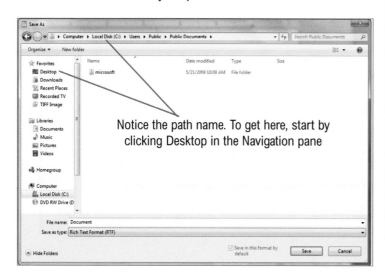

Notice the path name. To get here, start by clicking Desktop in the Navigation pane

3   Open any other folder that contains data you'd like to move or copy here.

4   Drag that folder all the way off the left side of the screen. It will reposition itself automatically on the left side of the Desktop.

5   Use the techniques you learned earlier in this chapter to right-click and drag and drop the data to move or copy from the folder on the left to the appropriate folder on the right.

Restoring folders (and files) from the Recycle Bin

Since you learned to delete files and folders in this chapter it's only fair to tell you how to recover them if you deleted them accidentally. Every file or folder you delete is sent to the Recycle Bin. Until the Recycle Bin is emptied, which you must do manually or using Disk Cleanup, you can 'restore' the file, which means you will put it back where it was before you deleted it.

Restore folders (and files) from the Recycle Bin

1 Double-click the Recycle Bin, it's on the Desktop.

2 Browse through the files, folders, shortcuts, pictures and other data. If you find something you did not mean to delete, right-click it.

3 Choose Restore from the drop-down list.

The Recycle Bin sits on the Desktop. Double-click it to open it.

If you find a file you want to restore (recover), right-click it and choose Restore. The file will reappear in the same location it was prior to deleting.

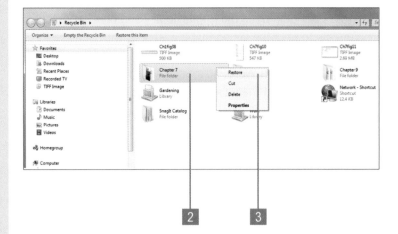

Jargon buster

Icon – a visual representation of a file or folder that you can click to open it.

Library – a top-level organisational folder.

Folder – a second-level organisational folder.

Subfolder – a third-level organisational folder you create.

Windows Live Mail

Windows Live Mail is the only thing you need to send and receive e-mail, manage your contacts, manage sent, saved and incoming e-mail, and send photo e-mail (which which we'll talk about later). Within Windows Live Mail you can also print e-mail, create folders for storing e-mail you want to keep, manage unwanted e-mail, open attachments, send pictures inside an e-mail, and more.

To use Windows Live Mail, you first need to download it. It's part of the Windows Live Essentials package, also called Windows Live. If you haven't downloaded it yet, return to Chapter 1 for instructions. Once Windows Live Mail is installed, you'll need an e-mail address and related information, all of which you can get from your ISP, Microsoft, Google or wherever you obtained your e-mail address. With this information to hand, you'll work through the Add an E-mail account wizard, inputting the required information when prompted, to set up the program. Once Live Mail is set up, you're ready to send and receive mail. Don't worry, it's easy!

What you'll do

Set up an e-mail address

Resolve errors

View an e-mail and open an attachment

Add the Print icon

Print an e-mail

Compose and send an e-mail

Reply to and forward an e-mail

Attach a picture or file using the Insert menu

Attach a picture or file by right-clicking

Add a contact

Send an e-mail to multiple recipients with Address Book

Create a new category

Configure Windows Live Mail junk e-mail options

Create a new folder

Clean Windows Live Mail

Setting up an e-mail address

To use Windows Live Mail you need to set up an e-mail address. This is first and foremost, and is done even before exploring the Mail interface. That's because the first time you use Windows Live Mail you'll be prompted to input the required information regarding your e-mail address and e-mail servers. When creating your first e-mail address (and any subsequent ones), you'll need to input the following information:

- E-mail address – Here's where you type the e-mail address you chose when you signed up with your ISP. It often takes this form: *yourname@yourispname.com*. E-mail addresses are not case-sensitive.

- Password – This is where you'll enter the password you chose when setting up your online account with your ISP. Passwords are case sensitive.

- Display Name – This is the name that will appear in the From field when you compose an e-mail, and in the sender's inbox (under From in their e-mail list) when they receive e-mail from you. Don't put your e-mail address here; put your first and last name, and any additional information. I use Joli Ballew, MVP.

- Mail Servers – This is where you'll enter the information your ISP gave you about its mail servers. Most often this includes a POP3 incoming mail server and an SMTP outgoing mail server. Often the server names look something like *pop.yourispnamehere.com* and *smtp.yourispnamehere.com*.

Set up an e-mail address

1. Click Start, and in the Search window, type Live Mail.

2. You should be prompted to set up an e-mail account automatically; if you aren't, click Add an E-mail Account. (You'll need to perform this step to create a secondary account, if you decide to do so.)

3. Type your e-mail address and password.

4. Type your Display Name.

5. Do not tick Manually configure server settings for e-mail account.

6. Click Next.

Did you know?

If you don't have an e-mail address yet, click Get a free e-mail account or call your Internet service provider.

For your information

If you want Windows Live Mail to remember your password, leave Remember password ticked.

Setting up an e-mail address (cont.)

7 If you receive the message shown here, stating you have successfully set up your account click Finish, and if prompted, Download. (If you do not see this message, skip to Step 8.)

8 If prompted, type the required information. You will have to call your ISP or visit its website to get this information.

9 Click Next.

10 If desired, select Set this account as the default mail account. You'll only see this option if you already have another e-mail account configured in Live Mail.

Did you know?

You can add a second e-mail account by clicking Add e-mail account.

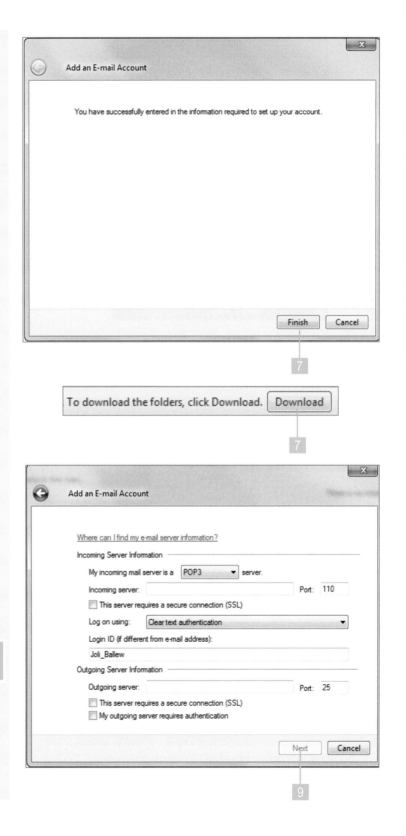

11 Click Finish.

12 As mail begins to arrive, you may see the prompt here. Click Please do not show me this dialogue again, and click Close. You'll learn about junk e-mail later in this chapter.

For your information

Send yourself an e-mail to see if you can send and receive without errors.

8

Important

If you get an error, read it carefully. It's most likely to be a typographical error you caused during set-up, an error stating that the outgoing server requires authentication (you'll need to tick the appropriate box), or perhaps that the password you typed is incorrect. Remember passwords are case sensitive.

You can resolve errors by editing the properties for an e-mail account. To edit the properties for any account, right-click the account name, and click Properties. The Properties dialogue box that opens will allow you to re-enter information including the e-mail address, password, name on the account, outgoing and incoming server names, and more.

Setting up an e-mail address (cont.)

Resolve errors

1. Right-click the name of the e-mail address to repair, and click Properties.

2. In the Properties dialogue box, browse through the tabs and repair the mistake. When in doubt, call your ISP. It is there to help.

3. Click OK.

For your information

Click Sync to test the settings. If you do not receive errors, at least the incoming e-mail server settings are correct.

Important

If you are repeatedly asked for a password even after inputting it, and you do not receive mail after doing so, you will need to review the properties for the account. Something is wrong with your settings.

Now that you have your e-mail address(es) set up, you can explore how Windows Live Mail organises your e-mail in the Folder List pane on the left side of the interface. There are several default folders, and you can add your own if desired.

- Unread e-mail – This holds e-mails you have yet to read in any other view.

- Unread from contacts – This holds e-mails from known contacts (those in your address book) that you've yet to read.

- Unread feeds – This holds e-mail from feeds you subscribe to like a news source or other website that updates content often. Click Feeds to view the feeds, and once there, click Manage Feeds to manage them.

- Inbox – This folder holds mail you've received.

- Drafts – This folder holds messages you've started, but not completed. Click File and click Save to put an e-mail in progress here.

- Sent items – This folder stores copies of messages you've sent.

- Junk e-mail – This folder holds e-mail that Windows Live Mail thinks is spam. You should check this folder occasionally since Mail may put e-mail in there you want to read.

- Deleted items – This folder holds mail you've deleted.

- Outbox – This folder holds mail you've written but have not yet sent.

Getting to know the Windows Live Mail interface (cont.)

At the bottom of the Folders pane are view options: Mail, Calendar, Contacts, Feeds, and Newsgroups. By default, Mail is selected. If you click another option, like Calendar, the interface changes.

Important

!

When you want to work with Mail, make sure Mail is selected in the bottom left of the interface. (Click Calendar to work with the Calendar, Contacts to work with Contacts, etc.)

You can configure Windows Live Mail so that the Deleted items folder empties every time you exit Windows Live Mail. But we won't suggest this. It's better to empty the Deleted items folder manually, because like the Recycle Bin, once it's emptied, the data is irretrievable. If you must though, you can configure Mail to empty on exit, from the Menus icon. Choose Options, and select the Advanced tab. Click Maintenance, and tick: 'Empty essages from the "Deleted items" folder on exit.' The defaults are shown right.

For your information

i

Explore the settings available from the Options dialogue box shown here. You'll find myriad ways to configure Windows Live Mail.

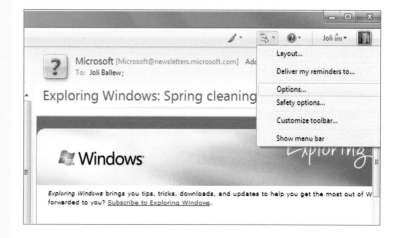

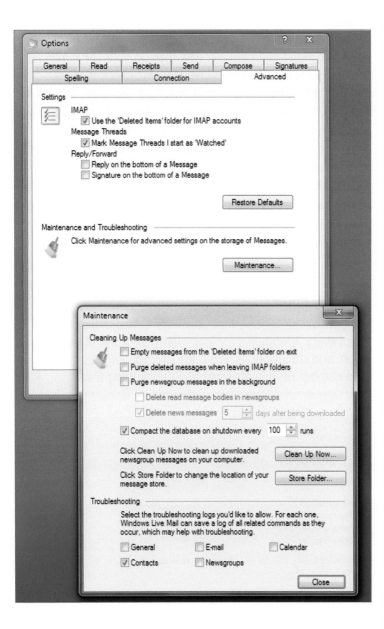

Receiving and viewing an e-mail

View an e-mail and open an attachment

1. In Windows Live Mail, click the Sync button to check for mail.

2. When new mail arrives, click it one time to read it in the Preview pane.

3. If the e-mail contains an attachment, you'll see a paperclip in both the Message pane and the Preview pane. To view the attachment, click once on the name of the attachment (next to the paperclip icon) in the Preview pane. If it's something that Windows Mail recognises and can preview, you'll see the preview in the Preview pane, as shown far right.

Each time you click the Sync button, Windows Live Mail checks to see if you have any new mail on your ISP's mail server. By default, Windows Live Mail will check every 30 minutes. When you receive mail, there are two ways to read it. You can click the message one time and read it in the Preview pane or double-click it to open it in its own window. Most people just click the e-mail one time, that way you don't have to close any windows after reading an e-mail (which is what you'd have to do if you double-clicked). You can also adjust the size of the panes by dragging the grey border between any of them up or down when using the Reading pane, which makes it even more convenient.

Did you know?

To have Windows Live Mail check for e-mail more often than every 30 minutes (or less often), click the Menus icon, and click Options. From the General tab, change the number of minutes from 30 to something else.

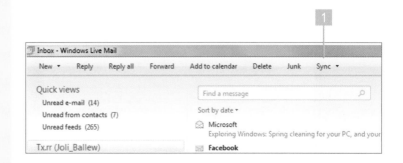

For your information

You may see a message that indicates pictures have been blocked to help prevent the sender from identifying your computer. You'll have to click the message to download pictures, but only do that if you know the sender and want to see the images.

4 If the e-mail attachment is a type of data that cannot be previewed in the Preview pane, when you click it once, nothing will happen. Double-click it to see an option to open it. You can also double-click any attachment to view it in a photo viewer, like Windows Live Gallery, shown here.

5 When prompted, click Open. *Never* open an attachment from someone you do not know! It could be a virus!

6 If you have a program installed on your computer that can open the attachment, it will open. If not, you'll receive an error. If you receive an error, you'll need to download and install a program that can open the attachment. Alternatively, you could reply to the sender and ask them to resend the attachment in another format.

Printing an e-mail

Sometimes you'll need to print an e-mail or its attachment. The e-mail could contain a receipt, a great joke you want to share with your friends who don't have or use e-mail or test results from a doctor. Whatever the case, Windows Live Mail makes it easy to print. Just check out the printer icon on the toolbar; click it once to print. (An e-mail has to be selected and a printer has to be installed to print.) After clicking the Print icon, the Print dialogue box will appear, where you can select a printer, set print preferences, choose a page range and, well, print.

If you do not see the Print icon on the toolbar, you'll have to add it.

Add the Print icon

1. Right-click an empty area of the toolbar and select Customize toolbar...

2. Under the Available buttons column, click Print.

3. Click the right arrow to add it to Current buttons column.

4. Click OK.

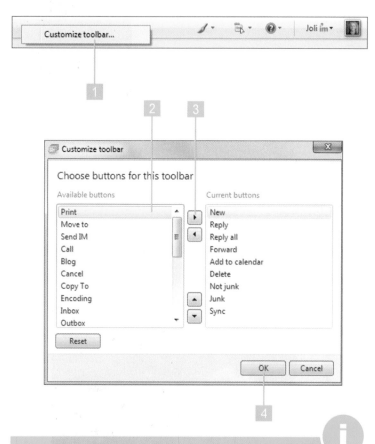

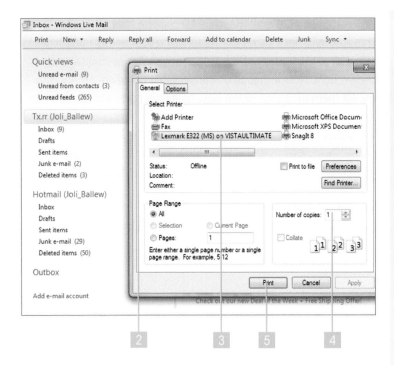

Print an e-mail

1. Select the e-mail to print by clicking it in the Message pane.

2. Click the Print icon.

3. In the Print dialogue box, select the printer to use, if more than one exists.

4. Configure additional options if desired, like number of copies.

5. Click Print.

8

For your information

You can configure print preferences and choose what pages to print using Preferences. Refer to your printer's user manual to find out what print options your printer supports.

Composing and sending an e-mail

You compose an e-mail message by clicking New on the toolbar. This icon sits right above the Folder bar. (Mail needs to be selected at the bottom of the Folder pane.) A new message is shown here. Notice that all of the available fields are empty. You will fill them in. Some of the New Message parts are labelled here.

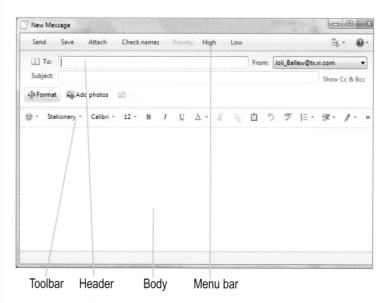

Toolbar   Header   Body   Menu bar

The header is where you input who the e-mail should be sent to, and the subject. The body is where you type the message. There's also a menu bar and a toolbar, which you can use to access other features, including tools you're already familiar with like Cut, Copy and Paste, spell check, font, font size, font colour, font style, and access to tools including Windows Contacts.

Here are some things to consider before and while you compose an e-mail:

- You'll need the e-mail address of the recipient; you'll type this into the 'To:' field. Alternatively, you can click the Address book icon to the left of 'To:' to choose it from your address book.

- To send the e-mail to more than one person, type their e-mail address and put a semicolon between each entry, like this: *joli@isp.com; bob@microsoft.com; kim@aol.com*. Alternatively, you can select the names from your address book, and Live Mail will insert the semicolons automatically.

- To send an e-mail to a group of people included in a category, type the name of the category. There are several you may want to choose from, including Family, Friends or Coworkers. To learn more about categories, refer to Working with categories, later in this chapter.

- If you want to send the e-mail to someone and you don't need them to respond, you can put them in the Cc line. Cc stands for carbon copy. (You can show this by clicking Show Cc & Bcc.)

- If you want to send the e-mail to someone and you don't want other recipients to know you included them in the e-mail, add them to the Bcc line. (You can show this by clicking Show Cc & Bcc.) Bcc stands for blind carbon copy and is a secret copy.

- Type the subject of the message in the 'Subject:' field. Make sure the subject adequately describes the body of your e-mail. Your recipients should be able to review the subject line later and be able to recall what the e-mail was about.

- Type the message in the body of the e-mail. Note that you can edit the data as you would in any word processing program – you can Cut, Copy and Paste, change the font, and more.

Beyond sending a 'new' e-mail, you can reply to an e-mail or forward it. Replying lets you send a response to the sender (you can reply to everyone if there are multiple recipients in the e-mail). Forwarding lets you send the entire e-mail to another person, which is often used to send an e-mail to someone not included in the e-mail you received. People spend a lot of time forwarding e-mails and, even though it's a common practice, beware. Most forwarded e-mails contain bad jokes, untrue information (hoaxes) or just plain junk you don't want to read. Do your part by limiting what you forward; just because you think it's true or funny doesn't make it so.

8

Composing and sending an e-mail (cont.)

Compose and send an e-mail

1. Verify that Mail is selected in the Folder pane, and click New.

2. In the To: field, type the e-mail address for the recipient or use the address book icon. If you want to add other names, separate each e-mail address with a semicolon.

3. Type a subject in the Subject field.

4. Type the message in the body pane.

5. Format the text as desired using the formatting tools shown.

6. Click Send.

Reply   Reply all   Forward

Reply to and forward an e-mail

1. Open an e-mail you've received and click Reply, Reply All, or Forward.

2. In the To field, type the e-mail address for the recipient. If you want to add other names, separate each e-mail address with a semicolon. Note that you can also type a category name, such as Friends or Family.

3. Type a subject in the Subject field.

4. Type the message in the body pane.

5. Format the text as desired using the formatting tools.

6. Click Send.

Attachments

Although e-mail that contains only a message serves its purpose quite a bit of the time, often you'll want to send a photograph, a short video, a sound recording, document or other data. When you want to attach something to your message other than text, it's called adding an attachment. There are many ways to attach something to an e-mail.

You can use the Attach button, for one. Then, you can browse to the location of the attachment, which will probably be in one of your personal folders. As with selecting and deleting multiple files in other scenarios, you can hold down the Ctrl key to select non-contiguous files, or the Shift key to select contiguous ones. The only problem with this method is that you have to be able to browse to the file you want to add. Sometimes, you won't be able to find it quickly or you won't know where it is. There are other ways to attach data.

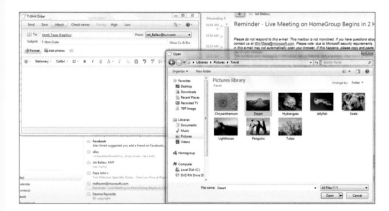

You can also right-click any file you want to attach, select Send to, and select Mail recipient (see top right). This method attaches the files to a new e-mail, which is fine if you want to create a new e-mail. The only problem with this is that it doesn't work if you'd rather send forwards or replies. This method only produces a new e-mail message. However, this method has a feature other methods don't. With it, you can resize any images you've selected before sending them. This is a great perk because many pictures are too large to send via e-mail, and resizing them helps manage an e-mail's size.

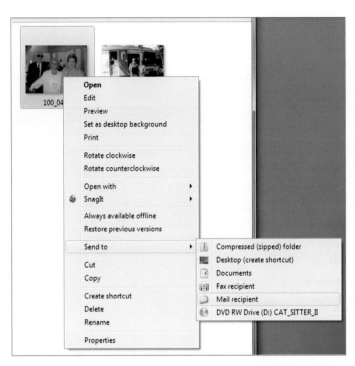

Important

Avoid sending large attachments, especially to people that you know have a dial-up modem or those that get e-mail only on a small device like a BlackBerry, iPhone or mobile PC. A video of your grandchildren or pets might take you only 8 seconds to send, but it can bog down a dial-up connection for hours.

8

You can also e-mail from within applications, such as Microsoft Word or Excel. Generally, you'll find the desired option under the File menu, as a submenu of Send, or from a button located in the top right-hand corner, and a submenu of Send. Other than having to open the file in the appropriate application, there is no disadvantage to using this method.

Attachments (cont.)

Attach a picture or file using the Insert menu

1 With Windows Live Mail open, click New.

2 In the New Message window, click Attach.

3 If necessary, resize the Open window so you can see the panes clearly, and the contents of the window.

4 In the left pane of the Open window, browse to the location of the file. You may need to:

a. Click Documents or Pictures under Libraries.

b. Expand Network and drill down to the appropriate folder, computer or user, if necessary.

c. Click Desktop under Favorites, as shown next.

5 Click the item to attach.

6 Click Attach.

7 Notice the attachment is shown in the new message.

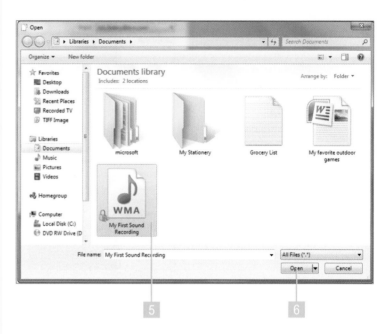

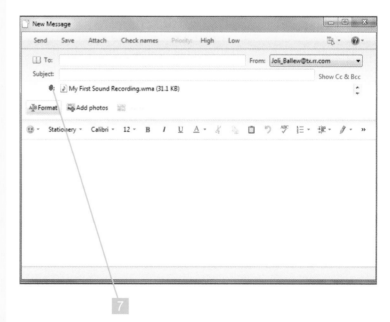

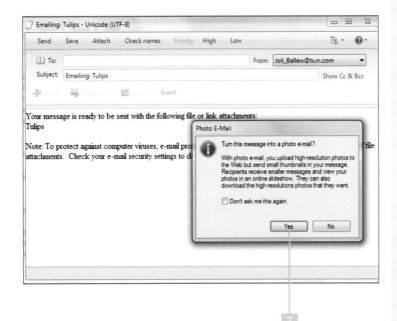

Attach a picture or file by right-clicking

1. Locate the picture or file to attach to a new e-mail message. You will probably have to open a folder, unless the file is stored on your Desktop.

2. Select and then right-click the file or picture.

3. Select Send to.

4. Click Mail recipient.

5. Select the appropriate size. Medium is shown here, but I prefer to receive e-mail at the Small size, 800 × 600. At this size they appear perfectly in Windows Live Mail.

6. Click Attach.

7. If prompted and if desired, click Yes to turn the message into a 'photo e-mail'. If you choose to do this, recipients will receive the e-mail with the picture inside the body of the e-mail, but they'll also be able to click Play slideshow to view full-size images on the Internet. Click No if you do not want to offer this option.

8. Compose the e-mail and click Send.

Important

If you receive an error message from Microsoft Outlook after clicking Attach, or if the picture causes Microsoft Outlook to open, it means that Microsoft Outlook is installed and is configured to be the default mail program. To change this behaviour, search for and open Set Default Programs, choose Windows Live Mail, and click Set this program as the default. Click OK.

Attachments (cont.)

Here's how the image might appear in the recipient's inbox. This image shows the e-mail in Windows Live Mail. Note the Play slideshow option. This option is available only if you choose to send the photo(s) in a photo e-mail, as noted in Step 7. On the right is the screen you'll see if you click Play slideshow. Note that the recipient can change the speed of the slideshow, manually move forward or back, download any picture(s), and even view the images in a larger size.

A Windows Live Mail contact is a data file that holds the information you keep about a person. You can think of it like a digital Rolodex. The contact information looks like a 'contact card', and the information can include a picture, e-mail address, mailing address, first and last name, and similar data. Here's the contact window.

Double-click any name to see the contact card. You can easily add data using the tabs offered. For instance, click Edit, then the Personal tab, to add a street address, country or region, phone and other information. There's even a Family tab where you can input birthdays, anniversaries and children's names.

Managing contacts

For your information

When someone gives you their e-mail address and other personal data, create a contact card for them. You'll learn how to do this on the next page.

8

Important

The best way to view your contacts and add new ones is from inside Windows Mail. At the bottom of the Folders pane, click Contacts.

Managing contacts (cont.)

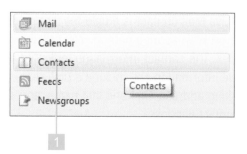

Add a contact

1. From Windows Live Mail, click the Contacts icon in the Folders pane or on the toolbar.

2. Click New. This will open the Add a Contact window.

3. Type all of the information you want to add. Be sure to add information to each tab.

4. Click Add contact.

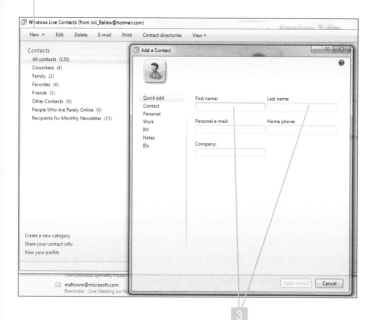

For your information

From the IM tab, type the contact's Windows Live Messenger address. That way, you'll be able to contact them through Windows Live Messenger, another Live application that's free.

Did you know?

You can click the arrow next to New to see additional options: Contact, Category, E-mail message, Photo e-mail.

For your information

After adding the contact, click All contacts and locate the contact. If desired, drag the contact card to a new category under All contacts. When you add a contact to a specific category, like Family, you make it easy to send an e-mail to everyone in that category.

If you forward jokes you receive via e-mail to your kids, friends and/or colleagues, you know each time you forward something you have to manually type each of your recipient's e-mail addresses for each e-mail you send. Alternatively, you can use your address book to add multiple users quickly. However, it's also possible to use an existing *category* of contacts or create a new *category* of contacts, and when you want to send an e-mail to everyone in the category, you need only select it. If you were familiar with groups in Windows Mail or Outlook Express, this is basically the same thing. Some categories have already been created for you, as you can see from the Contacts information. You can manually add people to a category by dragging their contact card from All contacts to the desired category.

Working with categories

Send an e-mail to multiple recipients with Address Book

1. In Windows Live Mail, click New.

2. To the left of the To box, click the Address Book icon.

3. Go through the list and double-click each contact you'd like to add to the To line. If you'd like to add an entire category, like Family, click Family.

4. Click OK to close the Address Book.

Did you know?

You can simply type Family into the To line to add it without using the Address Book.

Did you know?

Windows Live Mail already has a few categories configured. These include All contacts, Coworkers, Family, Favorites, Friends, Other Contacts and People Who Are Rarely Online. Contacts are automatically placed in these categories as you add them based on the information you input about them.

Working with categories (cont.)

Did you know?

You can type your own name in the To field, and put everyone else in the Bcc field. That way, you'll get a copy of the message you send and others won't be able to see who else received the e-mail or their personal e-mail addresses.

For your information

To add names to the Cc line or Bcc line, click Show Cc & Bcc. Click the Address book next to these lines. Click OK when finished.

Create a new category

1 In Windows Live Mail, click the Contacts icon.

2 Click the arrow next to New in the Contacts window, and click Category.

3 Type a category name.

4 Click a contact to add. As with selecting and deleting multiple files in other scenarios, you can hold down the Shift key to select contiguous contacts in the list.

5 When finished, click Save.

Did you know?

You can remove contacts from the category by selecting the contact and clicking Remove Selected Contacts.

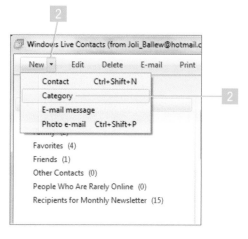

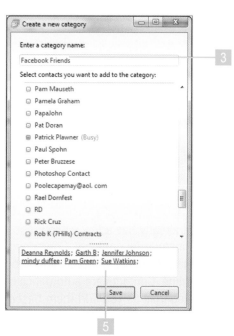

Just like you receive unwanted information from solicitors, radio stations, billboards, television ads, flyers, cinema ads and, the newest annoyance, television advertising crawlers that actually appear on some channels *while* you're watching a television show, you're going to get advertisements in e-mails. This is referred to as junk e-mail or spam. Unfortunately for you, there's no governing agency placing rules on what can and cannot be sent in an e-mail, as there is with television, radio and other transmission media. This means that not only are most of the advertisements scams and rip-offs but they also often contain pornographic images. Even if you were to purchase something via a spam e-mail, it's not guaranteed that the item will arrive or that it will meet any governmental quality requirements. And you can be sure that someone is more interested in having your credit card numbers than sending you an actual product.

Before you read any further, take note: never, and I mean never, buy anything from a junk e-mail, send money to a sick or dying person, send money for your portion of a lottery ticket, order medication, reply with bank account numbers, National Insurance numbers or any other personal information, believe that Bill Gates himself will pay you for forwarding an e-mail to friends, believe you'll have good luck (or bad) if you don't forward a message to friends or otherwise do anything but delete the e-mail. Do not attempt to unsubscribe from a mailing list, do not click Reply and do not perpetuate hoaxes.

That said, if you purposefully ask for a legitimate company to send you e-mail, perhaps Amazon.com, it's often OK to click on the link in the e-mail to visit the site. However, always make sure to check the web address once connected. Just because you click on a link in an e-mail to visit *www.amazon.com* doesn't mean you're going to get there. You might get to a site named *www.1234.amazon.com/validate your credit card number*, which would indeed be a scam. It's best to delete all spam. And that's all I have to say about that.

Unwanted e-mail (cont.)

There are a lot of options for reducing the amount of junk e-mail, or spam, you receive. First, don't give your e-mail address to any website, company or include it in any registration card, unless you're willing to receive junk e-mail from them and their partners. Understand that companies collect and sell e-mail addresses for profit. Don't get involved in that. Second, keep Mail's junk e-mail options configured as high as you can, and train it to filter unwanted e-mail automatically. With vigilance, you can keep spam to a minimum.

Mail's junk e-mail options

Windows Live Mail helps you avoid unwanted e-mail messages by catching evident junk e-mail and moving it to the Junk e-mail folder. You get to decide how strict Live Mail is, as you'll learn shortly. Additionally, you can block messages from specific e-mail addresses by adding them to the Blocked Senders list and prevent blocking of valid e-mail using the Safe Senders list.

There are four filtering options in Windows Live Mail:

- No Automatic Filtering – Use this only if you do not want Windows Live Mail to block junk e-mail messages. Windows Live Mail will continue to block messages from e-mail addresses listed on the Blocked Senders list.

- Low – Use this option if you receive very little junk e-mail. You can start here and increase the filter if it becomes necessary.

- High – Use this option if you receive a lot of junk e-mail and want to block as much of it as possible. Use this option for children's e-mail accounts. Note that some valid e-mail will probably be blocked, so you'll have to review the Junk e-mail folder occasionally, to make sure you aren't missing any e-mail you want to read.

- Safe List Only – Use this option if you only want to receive messages from people or domain names on your Safe Senders list. This is a drastic step and requires you to add every sender you want to receive mail from to the Safe Senders list. Use this as a last resort.

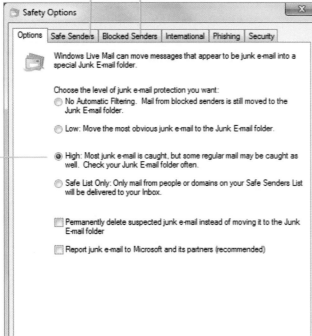

Configure Windows Live Mail junk e-mail options

1. Click the arrow next to the Menus icon.

2. Click Safety options.

3. From the Options tab, make a selection. We suggest starting at High and taking the time to 'train' Live Mail by checking the Junk e-mail folder often, at least at first.

4. Click the Safe Senders tab.

5. To add a person to the Safe Senders list, click Add and type their e-mail address. To add a domain, type the domain name. (Domain names include Amazon.com, Facebook.com or GeneralMotors.com.)

6. Click the Blocked Senders tab.

7. To add a person to the Blocked Senders list, click Add, and type their e-mail address. To add a domain, type the domain name. (Domain names include porn.com, hate.com and the like.)

For your information

Under the Blocked Senders tab, select both options at the bottom: Bounce the blocked messages back to the sender (the spammer will think it's reached an invalid address); and if the e-mail is a newsletter, unsubscribe from the mailing list.

Unwanted e-mail (cont.)

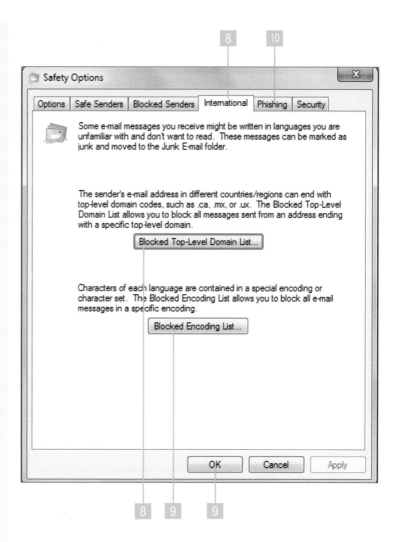

8 Click the International tab. Read the information offered and decide if you want to block domains from different countries. By blocking these domains, you will reduce the amount of spam you receive from other countries, in languages you do not understand. To configure this, click Blocked Top-Level Domain List. Then, select the countries to block. Click OK.

9 Click the International tab. Read the information offered and decide if you want to block specific character sets. You can block e-mail from various countries with this method. By blocking these encodings, you will reduce the amount of spam you receive from other countries, in languages you do not understand. To configure this, click Blocked Encoding List. Then, select the countries to block. Click OK.

10 Click the Phishing tab.

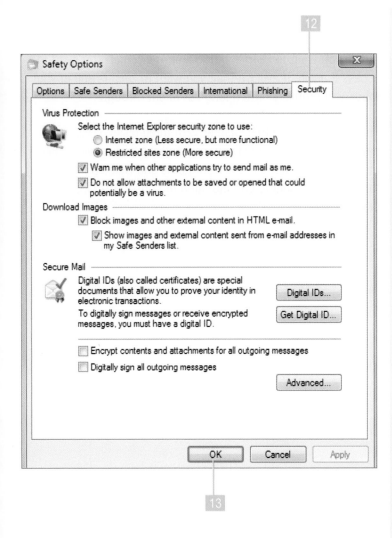

Unwanted e-mail (cont.)

11 Select Protect my Inbox from messages with potential Phishing links. Additionally, move phishing e-mail to the Junk e-mail folder.

12 Click the Security tab. The default settings are usually fine, but read through them to see if you'd like to make changes. The settings here are how I configure mine.

8

13 Click OK.

For your information

On the Security tab, you may want to select Internet Zone (less secure, but more functional), for a better web experience.

Keeping Windows Live Mail clean and tidy

It's important to perform some housekeeping chores once a month or so. If you don't, you may find it hard to manage the e-mail you want to keep and find an e-mail when you need to access it again; if every e-mail you want to keep is still in your Inbox you probably have a long list to sift through.

That said, we'll end this chapter with three tasks: creating a new folder to hold e-mail you want to keep and moving mail into it, deleting items in the Sent items and Deleted items folders, and changing configuration options in the Options dialogue box.

Create a new folder

1. In Windows Live Mail, click the arrow next to New.
2. Select Folder.

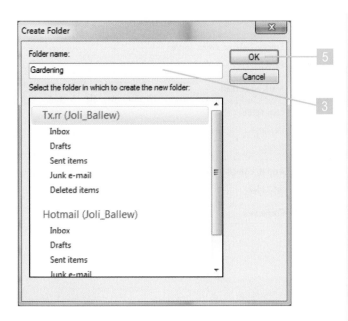

3 Type a name for the new folder.

4 If you have more than one e-mail account configured, select which folder you'd like the folder to be under in the list. Here, clicking Inbox under Tx.rr (Joli_Ballew) will cause a new folder to be added under Inbox, named Gardening.

5 Click OK.

6 Note the new folder in the Local Folders list.

7 To move any e-mail message to the new folder, select it (you probably have to click Inbox first) and drag it to the new folder. Drop it to complete the move.

Clean Windows Live Mail

1 Right-click Junk e-mail.

2 Click Empty 'Junk e-mail' folder.

3 Right-click Deleted Items.

Did you know?

Using the same technique, you can create subfolders inside folders you create.

Keeping Windows Live Mail clean and tidy (cont.)

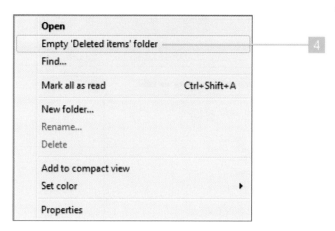

Open	
Empty 'Deleted items' folder	4
Find...	
Mark all as read	Ctrl+Shift+A
New folder...	
Rename...	
Delete	
Add to compact view	
Set color	▶
Properties	

4 Click Empty 'Deleted items' folder.

For your information

To delete a single e-mail in any folder, click the e-mail, and click Delete on the menu bar.

Internet Explorer

9

Introduction

Windows 7 comes with Internet Explorer 8, an application you can use to surf the Internet. Internet Explorer 8 is a 'web browser', and it has everything you need, including a pop-up blocker, zoom settings and accessibility options, as well as tools you can use to save your favourite web pages, set home pages and sign up for read RSS feeds and web slices. Internet Explorer has a feature called 'tabbed browsing' too. With tabs, you can have multiple web pages open at one time, without having multiple instances of Internet Explorer open and running. Accelerators are a new feature. When you highlight data on a page, an accelerator icon appears. Click it and you can perform tasks with the selected data including mapping an address, e-mailing the link, and more.

What you'll do

Open Internet Explorer

Explore tabbed browsing and surf the Internet

Set a home page

Mark a favourite

Organise favourites

Change the zoom level

View and clear History

Use accelerators

Print an entire web page

Print a selection from a web page

Configure website fonts and colours

Override website font and colour settings

Subscribe to RSS feeds

Work with RSS feeds

Use web slices

The Internet Explorer interface

Internet Explorer 8 – from here on referred to as IE8 – offers all of the tools you'll need to surf the Internet. As with other applications, it has toolbars and icons where you can access everything you need to perform Internet-related tasks. You can save links to your most often accessed websites, use tabs to open multiple websites at the same time, and type words into a Search window to help you locate anything at all on the web. There's also RSS for subscribing to websites that offer an RSS feed (which allows you to download only current information for the site, which is often news headlines, new articles or new travel discounts), and better security than ever. Finally, there are accelerators, a new way to work with selected data.

You can open IE8 a number of ways. On the Taskbar, look for the big blue E. Click it once to open the program. You can also open Internet Explorer from the Start menu, from the All Programs list. It's near the top.

As you can see here, there are several parts to the Internet Explorer interface. These include but are not limited to:

- Address bar – Used to type in Internet addresses, also known as URLs (universal resource locators). Generally, an Internet address takes the form of:
http://www.companyname.com

- Command bar – Used to access icons such as the Home and Print icons. See Table 9.1 for a list of icons and their uses.

- Tabs – Used to access websites when multiple sites are open.

- Search window – Used to search for anything on the Internet.

- Status bar – Used to find information about the current activity.

- Favorites tab – Used to access your list of saved websites, called Favorites.

Did you know?

Because IE8 uses new technologies for obtaining web data, if you come across a website that does not look or 'act' the way you think it should, you can click Compatibility View Settings under the Tools menu.

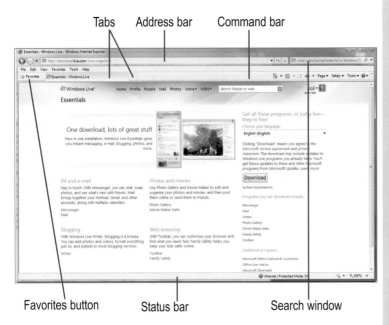

Tabs Address bar Command bar

Favorites button Status bar Search window

Note: Throughout this chapter you'll learn how to use these and other features of Internet Explorer; all you need to learn from this image are the names of the interface features.

9

The Internet Explorer interface (cont.)

Table 9.1 Command bar icons from left to right

Command bar icon	What it does
Favorites	View favourites you've added, RSS feeds and browsing history.
Tabs	Access open tabs.
Home	Accesses your home page (or home pages). This icon includes a drop-down menu too, which lets you change your home page(s) and add and remove home page(s). (It's the icon that looks like a house.)
Add web slices or use RSS	Click to get access to changing content on the current web page.
Get mail	Provides access to Windows Live Mail if it is installed.
Print	Lets you print a web page (or part of one).
Page	Offers a drop-down menu that allows access to features such as zoom and text size. You can also send a copy of the page you're viewing as an e-mail attachment using Windows Live, if it is installed.
Safety	Offers a drop-down list that lets you delete your browsing history, view security reports, read a website's privacy policy, and more.
Tools	Offers a drop-down menu that lets you access security feature configuration, Internet options and personalisation options.
Help	Offers a drop-down menu that is similar to the Help menu item in the Classic Menu. (It's the question mark icon.)
Blog this	Allows you to blog about the current page using Windows Live Writer, if it is installed. You may have to click the arrow, as shown next to the Help icon in the screenshot on the previous page).

Locating a website

Your first order of business is to type in a URL and go to a website. URLs and website names (as far as we're concerned right now), start with *http://www*. I don't want to go into detail about why this is, but suffice it to say, in almost all instances you'll need to type this first. After the *www.*, you'll type the website's name. Often this is the name of the company, like Amazon or Microsoft, and its ending, which is often *.com*, *.edu*, *.gov*, *.org* or *.net*.

?

Did you know?

.com is the most popular website ending, and it means the website is a company, business or personal website. *.edu* is used for educational institutions, *.gov* for government entities, *.org* for non-profit organisations (mostly) and *.net* for miscellaneous business and companies or personal websites. There are others though, including *.info*, *.biz*, *.tv* and *.uk.com*.

Here are some examples of websites you can type into the address bar:

- *http://www.microsoft.com/uk*
- *http://www.amazon.com*
- *http://www.greatbritain.com*

?

Did you know?

When a website name starts with *https://*, it means it's secure. When purchasing items online, make sure the payment pages have this prefix.

9

The Internet Explorer interface (cont.)

Jargon buster

There are a few words you're going to see often, including URL, link, website, and others. To get the most out of this chapter, you need to know what these mean. Here are some terms you should know before continuing:

Domain name – for our use here, a domain name is synonymous with a website name.

Favorite – a web page that you've chosen to maintain a shortcut for in Favorites.

Home page – the web page that opens when you open IE8. You can set the home page and configure additional pages to open as well.

Link – a shortcut to a web page. Links are often offered in an e-mail, document or web page to allow you to access a site without having to actually type in its name. In almost all instances, links are underlined and in a different colour than the page they are configured on.

Load – a web page must 'load' before you can access it. Some pages load instantly while others take a few seconds.

Navigate – the process of moving from one web page to another or viewing items on a single web page. Often the term is used as follows: 'click the link to navigate to the new web page'.

Search – a term used when you type a word or group of words into a Search window. Searching for data produces results.

Scroll up and scroll down – the process of using the scroll bars on a web page or the arrow keys on a keyboard to move up and down the pages of a website.

Website – a group of web pages that contain related information. Microsoft's website contains information about Microsoft products, for instance.

URL – The information you type to access a website, like *http://www.microsoft.com*.

Tips for using IE8

There are a few tips and tricks when using IE8. The first one I want to mention applies to typing in a website using the Address bar. You'll want to commit this key combination to memory: Ctrl+Enter. Here's how it works: Instead of typing, say, *http://www.microsoft.com* into the Address bar, just type 'Microsoft'. Then, hold down the Ctrl key on the keyboard and press the Enter key. IE8 will automatically add the *http://www* to the beginning and *.com* to the end!

There are several key combinations you might want to use once you've navigated to a website. Keyboard shortcuts are shown in Table 9.2.

The Internet Explorer interface (cont.)

Table 9.2 Keyboard shortcuts	
Keyboard shortcut	**What it does**
Alt+left arrow key	Go to the previous page visited in the current tab.
Alt+right arrow key	Go forward to a page visited in the current tab.
Esc	Stop the current page from loading.
Alt+Home	Go to your home page.
Ctrl+Enter	Automatically add *www* and *.com* to what you typed in the Address bar.
Alt+F4	Close the current tab.
Ctrl+D	Add the current page to your Favorites list.
Shift+mouse click	Open a link in a new window.
Ctrl+mouse click	Open a link in a new background tab.
Ctrl+Shift+mouse click	Open a link in a new foreground tab.
Ctrl+T	Open a new tab.
Ctrl+Tab	Switch between available tabs.
Ctrl+(+)	Zoom page by 10 per cent.
Ctrl+(-)	Decrease page zoom by 10 per cent.
Ctrl+0	Zoom to 100 per cent (normal view).

9

The Internet Explorer interface (cont.)

Three ways to open Internet Explorer

1 Click the blue 'e' icon on the Taskbar.

2 Click Start, All Programs, Internet Explorer.

3 Click the blue 'e' icon on the Taskbar and drag it upwards. A menu like the one shown here will appear. You can then click any website in the list to open IE8 and go directly to that site.

Explore tabbed browsing and surf the Internet

1 With Internet Explorer open, drag your mouse over the address currently showing on the Address bar. Do this even if the Address bar shows about:blank. The contents of the Address bar should appear blue.

2 Type the following: *http://www.microsoft.com/uk*

3 Use the scroll bars to view the entire web page.

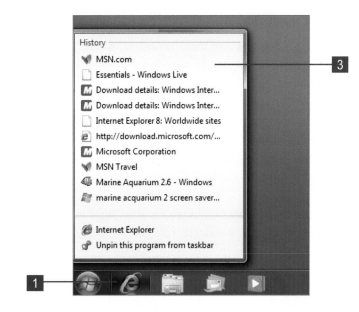

Did you know?

IE8 is pinned to the Taskbar. You can remove it by right-clicking and selecting Unpin this program from taskbar. To 'repin' it, right-click Internet Explorer (from the Start, All programs menu) and select Pin to Taskbar.

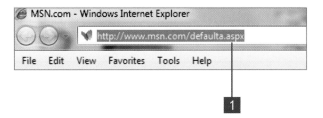

Did you know?

You can also highlight only the part of the address that appears after *http://www.* and leave the unhighlighted parts of the address intact.

Did you know?

If you can't see the Menu bar – the one with File, Edit, View, etc. – click the Alt key once on your keyboard.

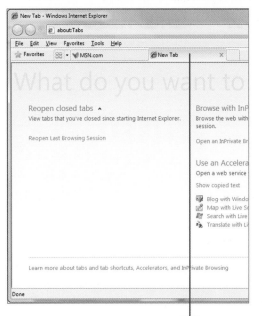

The Internet Explorer interface (cont.)

4 Look for a link named Support. When you hover your mouse over the word Support, the mouse icon will change to a hand. (Web pages change often, so you might not see Support exactly where it's shown here. If you can't find Support, click any link.)

5 Notice your Support options. Click Help & Support Home. (Again, web pages change, so this may not be exactly what you see.)

6 Read and browse the page as desired.

7 Using your keyboard, hold down the Ctrl key and then press the letter 'T'. A new tab will appear.

8 In the new tab's Address bar, type 'amazon'.

9

The Internet Explorer interface (cont.)

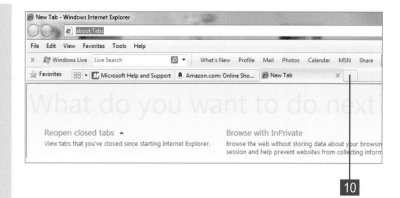

9　Hold down the Ctrl key, and press Enter. Notice the *http://www.* and *.com* are added automatically and the website opens.

10　Click the blank tab at the end of the open tab.

11　Type 'London' in the Address bar.

12　Click Enter on the keyboard.

13　Use the scroll bars to view any one of the listed websites.

14　Click the Quick Tabs button. It's located to the left of the first tab, and has four squares on it.

15　Notice all of your open pages are shown on a single page. Click any page to go to the web page.

16　Click the X in the top right-hand corner of IE8.

17　If you're prompted to close all open tabs, click Yes.

There are many more ways to personalise IE8 than we have room to detail here. However, there are a few things you will certainly want to know how to do, including adding a home page or multiple home pages, adding and organising favourites, and using the Zoom feature.

Designating home pages

You may recall that the earliest versions of Internet Explorer let you mark a web page as your home page, and that page would be displayed each time you opened the program. Starting with Internet Explorer 7, you can now assign multiple web pages as home pages. With multiple pages marked, when you start IE8, each website automatically loads in its own tab.

There are a number of ways to assign web pages as home pages, but you should always navigate to the pages first. Once you've opened a web page you want to add as a home page, click the arrow next to the Home button and choose Add or Change Home Page... You can then choose from three options:

- Use this webpage as your only home page – Select this option if you only want one page to serve as your home page.

- Add this webpage to your home page tabs – Select this option if you want this page to be one of several home pages.

- Use the current tab set as your home page – Select this option if you've opened multiple tabs and you want all of them to be home pages.

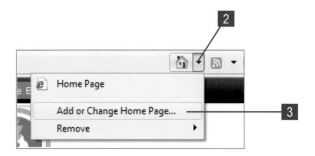

Personalise Internet Explorer

Set a home page

1 In IE8, use the Address bar to locate a web page you want to use as your home page.

2 Click the arrow next to the Home icon.

3 Click Add or Change Home Page.

9

Personalise Internet Explorer (cont.)

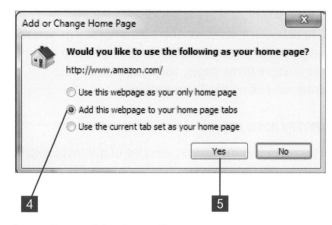

4 Make a selection using the information provided regarding each option.

5 Click Yes.

6 Repeat these steps as necessary.

Saving and organising favourites

Favourites are websites you save links to for accessing more easily at a later time. They differ from home pages because, by default, they do not open when you start IE8. The favourites you save appear in the Favorites Center, which you can access by clicking the yellow star on the Command bar. You will see some Favorites listed, including Microsoft Websites and MSN Websites. You can use the Favorites Center to quickly access your favourites, places you've recently visited and any RSS feeds you've subscribed to: they're all accessible from one location. Every time you save a favourite, it will appear here.

? Did you know?

You can also access favourites from the Favorites menu (which you can access by pressing Alt on the keyboard), if you're a fan of menus.

In addition to holding links to your favourite websites, the Favorites Center also includes access to History and Feeds. Feeds contain links to RSS feeds to which you've subscribed. History lists the links to the web pages you visited recently. Take a look at the History list here.

When adding favourites, you have two options. You can either add a single web page as a favourite or add a group of web pages to create a tab group of favourites.

Personalise Internet Explorer (cont.)

Mark a favourite

1. Go to the web page (or web pages) you want to configure as a favorite (or group of favourites).

2. Click the Favorites icon.

3. To add a single web page as a favourite, click Add to Favorites. To add all open websites (every tab that's open) as a tab group, click the arrow by Add to Favorites and select Add Current Tabs to Favourites.

4. Type a Folder Name, or a tab group name, when prompted.

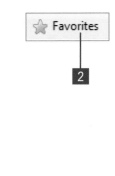

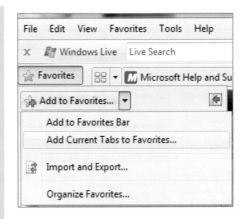

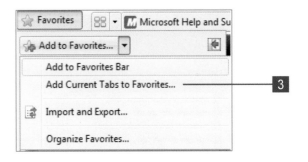

5   If you are saving a single web page, in the Create in drop-down list, select a folder to save the Favorite to. If you don't see a folder you like, click New Folder instead.

6   Click Add.

7   If you are saving a tab group, type a tab group name, called a Folder Name.

8   Leave Create in set to Favorites. (This will create a new tab group in the Favorites folder that contains links to all of the pages in your group.)

9   Click Add.

There will probably come a time when your Favorites Center becomes unwieldy. Perhaps you haphazardly saved favourites and now need to organise them or maybe you have favourites you want to delete. You may even have favourites you want to move to another folder. You can do this inside the Favorites Center by dragging and dropping files between folders. A better way is to open the Favorites folder inside your personal Documents library. That's because each time you make a change in the Favorites Center, it closes. This does not happen with the Favorites folder.

Organise favourites

1   Click Start.

2   Click your personal folder. That's the folder with your name on it.

3   Double-click the Favorites folder to open it.

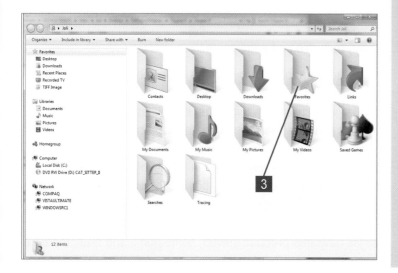

Personalise Internet Explorer (cont.)

4 Resize the icons so you can see them.

5 Click any subfolder under Favorites to see its contents.

6 To delete an entire subfolder, right-click it and choose Delete. This will delete the subfolder and all of its contents.

7 When prompted, click Yes.

8 To move a Favorite link from one subfolder to another, right-click it, choose Cut, and then repeat to paste the favourite in another folder.

9 Repeat these steps as necessary.

10 Click the X in the top right-hand corner of the Favourites folder to close it.

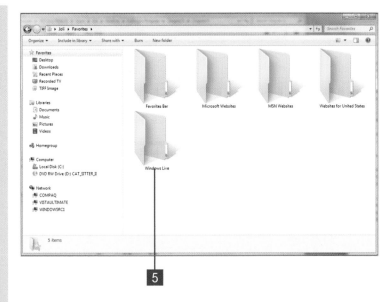

5

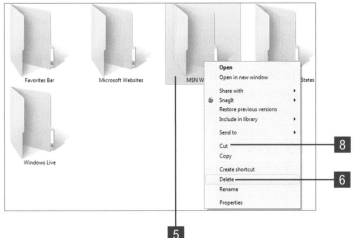

5

8

6

For your information ⓘ

In the Favourites folder you can also right-click any single link to delete it.

Using text size and page zoom

If you have trouble reading what's on a web page because the text is too small (or your eyes are too old), you can make the text larger in two ways. First, you can access the Text Size options from the View menu and choose from Largest, Larger, Medium (the default), Smaller, and Smallest. If you can't see the View menu, tap the Alt key on the keyboard to make it visible. This option works OK, but it can change the layout of the web page if it causes the text to become so large that it runs over images or other text on the page. Although most web pages have this problem solved, some don't, and thus, there's a better way to zoom in on a page.

I prefer the Zoom feature. Zoom intelligently zooms in on the entire page, which maintains the page's integrity, layout and look. The Zoom options are located under the View menu on the Command bar, but it's much easier to use the link at the bottom right of the browser window, on the Status bar. Just click it to show zoom options.

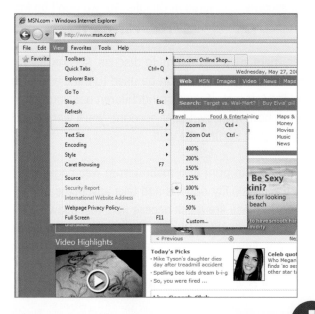

For your information

If you don't see this menu bar shown here, click the Alt key on the keyboard. It will appear.

In the task, we'll stick with the Zoom options on the Status bar.

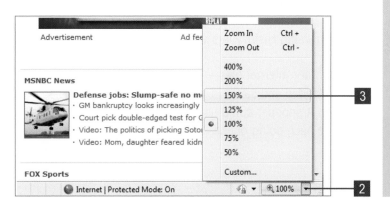

Change the zoom level

1 Open Internet Explorer and browse to a web page.

2 Click the arrow located at the bottom right of the Status bar to show the Zoom options.

3 Click 150%.

4 Notice how the web page text and images increase in size. Use the scroll bars to navigate the page.

For your information

The Status bar runs across the bottom of IE8. Look at the bottom right of the interface for the Zoom option.

9

Working with Internet Explorer

There's a lot going on behind the scenes in IE8, and a lot of it is security related. There's a pop-up blocker to keep unwanted ads from appearing when you visit web pages configured with them, and there are preconfigured security zones and privacy settings to help protect against any other threats you may run across while surfing the web. Since much of this is preconfigured, and because security is covered in Chapter 10, we won't go into the details much here regarding those features.

However, there are a few things to discuss, specifically cleaning up IE8 by deleting files that can be used to trace where you've been on the Internet. If your grandchildren use your computer, and do not have their own user account, you'll want to do this before they start surfing the web.

You'll also want to print information from web pages and configure accessibility options and take advantage of accelerators. These are quick access lists that allow you to perform tasks with selected data, like e-mail it, map it or even blog about it. Finally, you can print web pages or selections and make websites easier to see and use with accessibility options. We'll cover all of this next.

Deleting your web footprint

If you don't want people to be able to snoop around on your computer and find out what sites you've been visiting, first, create a password-protected user account for yourself. If you're worried beyond that or if you don't always log off when you've finished using the computer, you'll want to use a new feature called Delete Browsing History. Delete Browsing History is located under the Safety menu.

Delete Browsing History lets you delete the following files:

■ Temporary Internet files – These are files that have been downloaded and saved in your Temporary Internet Files folder. A snooper could go through these files to see what you've been doing online.

- Cookies – These are small text files that include data that identifies your preferences when you visit particular websites. Cookies are what allows you to visit, say, *www.amazon.com* and be greeted with 'Hello <your name>, We have recommendations for you!' Cookies help a site offer you a personalised web experience.

- History – This is the list of websites you've visited and any web addresses you've typed. Anyone can look at your History list to see where you've been.

- Form data – Information that's been saved using Internet Explorer's autocomplete form data functionality. If you don't want forms to be filled out automatically by you or someone else who has access to your PC and user account, delete this.

- Passwords – Passwords that were saved using Internet Explorer autocomplete password prompts.

- InPrivate Filtering data – Data that has been saved to detect where websites may be automatically sharing details about your visit.

Note: You also have the option to preserve your favourites and website data like cookies and temporary Internet files that you've input and want to keep, like those you use at Amazon or other sites you've saved.

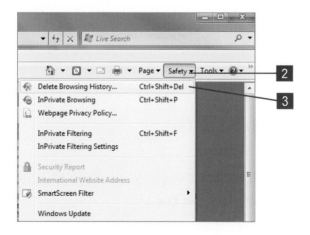

View and clear History

1 Open Internet Explorer.

2 Click Safety.

3 Click Delete Browsing History...

9

Working with Internet Explorer (cont.)

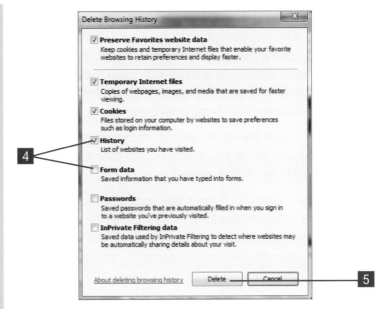

4 To accept the defaults for all of the listed items, click the Delete button. Otherwise, select and deselect as desired.

5 Click Delete.

Using accelerators

One of the most common tasks you'll do in IE8 is to copy data from a web page. You'll copy an address and then paste that address into a mapping website to obtain a route. You'll copy a map and then paste it into an e-mail to send to someone else. You may even copy data from one website and then go to another to find its meaning. Accelerators let you perform these most common copy and paste tasks more quickly.

There are many accelerators and web designers can create their own. Some of the more common accelerators include:

- Blog with Windows Live.
- Define with Encarta.
- E-Mail with Windows Live.
- Map with Live Search.
- Search with Live Search.
- Translate with Windows Live.
- Find more Accelerators.

To access an accelerator, highlight any data on a web page and then click the accelerator icon.

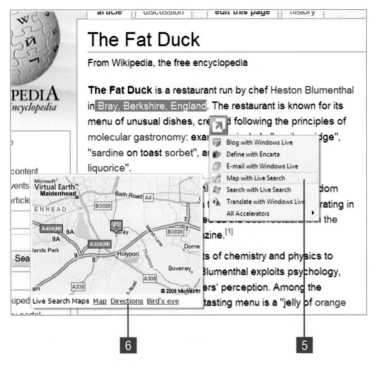

The Fat Duck is a restaurant run by chef Heston Blumenthal in Bray, Berkshire, England. The restaurant is known for its menu of unusual dishes, created following the principles of molecular gastronomy: examples include "snail porridge", "sardine on toast sorbet", and "salmon poached with liquorice".

Use accelerators

1. Open any web page in IE8.
2. Copy any data on the page.
3. Locate the accelerator icon.
4. Click the accelerator icon.
5. Click any option. Here I've selected Map with Live Search. Note the map.
6. If desired, click the map for additional directions.

For your information 9

For best results, download and install Windows Live Essentials. See Chapter 1.

Printing

Printing features are accessed, of all places, from the Print icon on the Command bar. Clicking the Print icon one time will print the page from the PC's default printer. You won't be able to set options (although it's somewhat probable that the same options you configured last time will still apply). Clicking the arrow next to the Print icon offers the menu shown overleaf; clicking the Print icon will take you directly to the Print dialogue box.

Working with Internet Explorer (cont.)

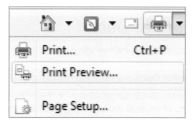

There are three menu options under the Print icon:

- Print... – Clicking Print opens the Print dialogue box where you can configure the page range, select a printer, change page orientation, change print order and choose a paper type. Additional options include print quality, output bins and more. Of course, the choices offered depend on what your printer offers. If your printer can only print at 300 x 300 dots per inch, you can't configure it to print at a higher quality.

- Print Preview... – Clicking Print Preview opens a window where you can see before you print what the printout will actually look like. You can switch between portrait and landscape views, access the Page Setup dialogue box, and more.

- Page Setup... – Clicking Page Setup opens the Page Setup dialogue box. Here you can select a paper size, source, and create headers and footers. You can also change orientation and margins, all of which are dependent on what features your printer supports.

You'll use these options as desired to print web pages.

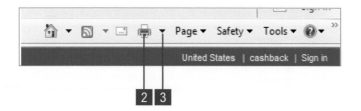

2 3

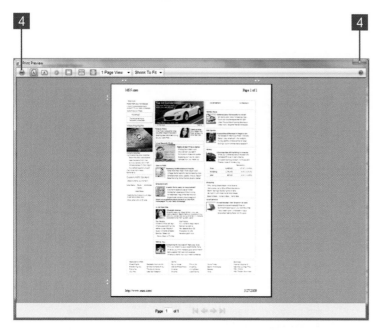

4   4

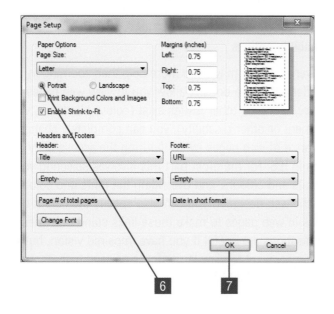

6   7

Working with Internet Explorer (cont.)

Print an entire web page

1 Locate a page on the Internet you'd like to print.

2 To print the page without configuring any print options or preferences, click the Print icon.

3 To see how the page will look after it's printed, click the down arrow next to the Print icon and choose Print Preview.

4 If you are happy with the way it looks, click the Print icon. If you do not like the way it appears, click the X in the top right-hand corner to close the window and skip to Step 5.

5 Click the arrow next to the Print icon and click Page Setup.

6 In the Page Setup dialogue box, make the desired selections.

7 Click OK.

9

Working with Internet Explorer (cont.)

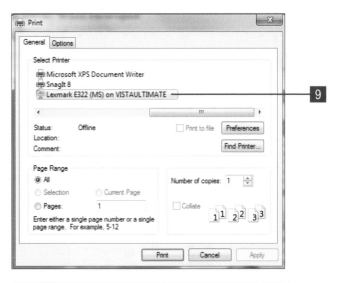

8 Click the arrow next to the Print icon and choose Print.

9 If you have more than one printer, you'll need to choose the printer and set other printer options before clicking Print.

Print a selection from a web page

1 Locate a page on the Internet you'd like to print.

2 If you do not want to print the entire web page, which often includes advertisements and unnecessary data, use your mouse to highlight what you want to print.

3 Right-click the selected text or data and click Print...

4 In the Page Setup dialogue box, click the down arrows to apply a paper size, source, and other options.

5 Under Page Range, click Selection.

6 Click Print.

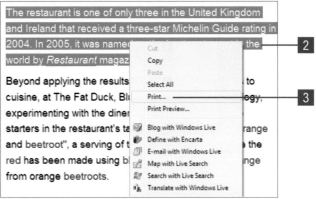

Accessibility options

Your over-50s eyes may need more help than zooming in on a page offers. If Zoom doesn't allow you to view web pages effectively, because other issues exist (colour blindness, visual impairment or other disability), you can completely change the appearance of web pages by configuring the accessibility options in IE8. For the most part this involves selecting your own fonts and colours, and overriding the fonts and colours set by the web designer. You can also specify the colour used for links in web pages to make those links stand out. These customisations are useful if you have impaired vision, but also if you simply want to view larger fonts or need high-contrast colours. Accessibility options are located in Internet Options, which you will open from the Tools menu.

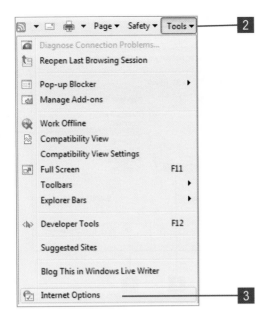

Configure website fonts and colours

1 Open Internet Explorer.

2 Click Tools.

3 Click Internet Options.

4 Click the General tab if it is not already selected.

5 Click Fonts.

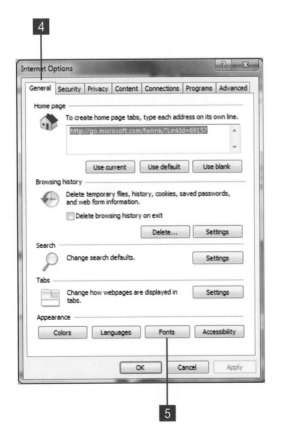

Working with Internet Explorer (cont.)

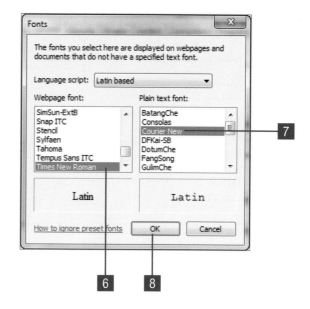

6　Select the Webpage font to use by selecting it in the list.

7　Select the Plain text font to use by selecting it from the list.

8　Click OK

9　Click Colors. (Back at the General tab.)

10　Clear the Use Windows colors tick box.

11　Click any colour box.

12　Select a colour and click OK.

13　Continue selecting colours until you are finished.

14　Click OK.

15　Click OK.

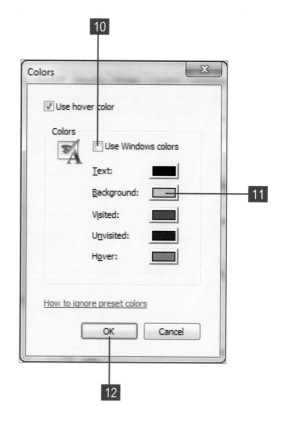

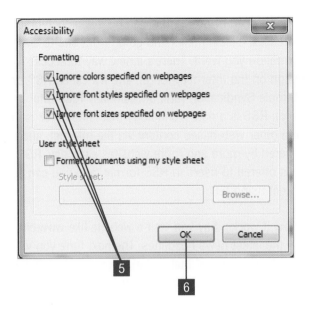

Override website font and colour settings

1 Open Internet Explorer.

2 Click Tools.

3 Click Internet Options.

4 Click Accessibility.

5 Tick Ignore colors specified on webpages, Ignore font styles specified on webpages, and Ignore font sizes specified on webpages boxes.

6 Click OK.

7 Click OK.

9

Exploring RSS

So far you've been browsing the web by manually typing in web addresses, clicking links and going from site to site to find the information you want. There's a new way to access information on the Internet though, and it's called RSS or Really Simple Syndication (and occasionally Rich Site Summary). RSS is a new technology that is used for issuing news and other web-based content via the Internet, and is being offered by more and more websites each day. RSS content is offered to users in RSS format, and you can access that content using IE8.

Here's how it works. Say you visit a website like *www.cnn.com* and read the latest news headlines. The next time you visit the site you will see some of that material again and you'll have to wade through it to access information you have yet to see or information that's been recently added. What RSS feeds do is let you 'subscribe' to RSS data, and the feed you subscribe to will be updated automatically on your PC and will only acquire information you've yet to view. When you view the feed, everything is new and you no longer have to pick through information you've already seen.

To get started with RSS, you'll need to locate the orange Feeds button on the Command bar in IE8. This button will only turn orange when you're visiting a website that offers at least one RSS feed. If it's grey, it's useless – no RSS feeds here. *www.cnn.com* offers at least one RSS feed and, thus, the RSS icon turns orange. Take a look.

To see the available RSS feed for a site, click the arrow next to the orange RSS icon. There are two feeds available from cnn.com: Top Stories and Recent Stories (see right). To subscribe to a feed, click it. You'll be transported to a web page that allows you to subscribe. To complete the process, just click Subscribe to this feed link.

You'll have the opportunity to name the feed in a familiar window that looks almost exactly like the Favorites window. Just like Favorites, you can create new folders and organise feeds. Once you've subscribed, the Feeds view changes to indicate that you've effectively subscribed to the feed and offers a View my feeds link. As with Favorites, you access your subscribed feeds through the Favorites Center.

There's one site I particularly like, *http://www.telegraph.com.uk*. Perform a search for Telegraph RSS feeds and check out the results. Here you can see links to all kinds of RSS feeds from news to politics to Manchester United. Select a feed and subscribe to it.

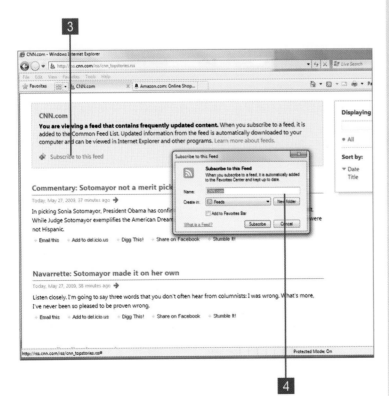

Subscribe to RSS feeds

1 Browse to a website that offers an RSS feed. Try *www.cnn.com*, a local newspaper's website, technical sites or your favorite website.

2 When you see an orange RSS icon on the Command bar, click it.

3 Click Subscribe to this feed to subscribe.

4 Type a name for the feed.

5 Use the drop-down list for Feeds to select an existing folder in which to save the feed or select New folder.

6 If you select New folder, type a name for the folder and click Create.

7 Click Subscribe.

9

For your information

For more information review the Favorites section earlier in this chapter.

Exploring RSS (cont.)

Work with RSS feeds

1 Click the yellow star icon to open the Favorites Center.

2 Click Feeds if it isn't already selected.

3 View the feeds by expanding folder names if necessary.

4 To view a feed, select it.

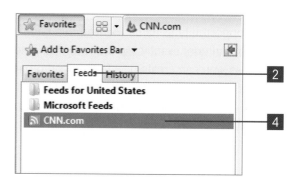

Web slices are a new feature of IE8. Using web slices, you can stay up to date without having to manually check frequently-changing data like the weather or new e-mail. If a web slice is available on a web page, a green web slice icon will appear on the Command bar where the orange RSS feed usually sits. Clicking the green web slice icon lets you see what slices are available and allows you to subscribe to them. When new information becomes available, the web slice will become highlighted, pointing to the information that's changed on the page. Web slices are becoming more and more popular, and offer a convenient way to keep up with every-changing web pages, specifically those with bid information, weather, e-mail, stocks, etc.

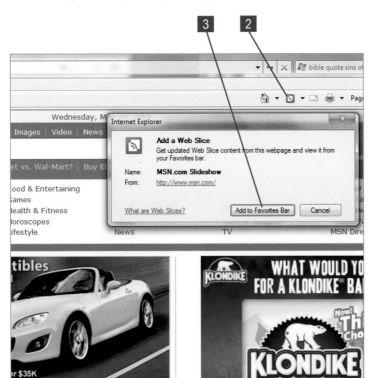

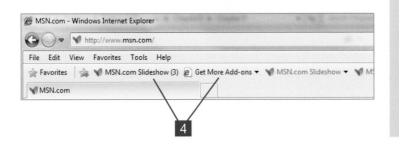

Exploring web slices

Use web slices

1 Locate a web page that offers web slices. Try *www.msn.com*.

2 Locate the green web slice icon on the Command bar and click it.

3 To add the web slices for the page, click Add to Favorites Bar.

4 Note the new items on the Favorites bar, which runs across the top of the MSN tab. Here you can see Get More Add-ons and MSN.com Slideshow.

9

For your information

When there's something new on the web slice you haven't seen, it darkens. After you click it, it lightens.

Staying secure

Introduction

Windows 7 comes with a lot of built-in features to keep you and your data safe from Internet ills, nosy children and download-happy grandchildren. Windows 7 also offers help in avoiding e-mail and web criminals whose only purpose in life is to steal your data, get your bank account or credit card numbers, or obtain your identity. Mail even informs you if it thinks an e-mail is 'phishing' for information you shouldn't give out.

Now, your reaction to these statements may be that you feel I've exaggerated the actual computer threats you may encounter or it may make you not want to share your computer, go online or read e-mail ever again. Whatever the case, it's important to understand there are threats out there, and Windows 7 does its best to offer you protection. If you take advantage of the available safeguards, you'll be protected in almost all cases. You just need to be aware of the dangers, heed warnings when they are given and use all of the available features in Windows 7 to protect yourself and your PC.

What you'll do

Add a new user account

Find out if you're logging on using an administrator account

Move from an administrator to a standard account

Require passwords

Use System Restore

Configure Windows Update

Use Windows Firewall

Use Windows Defender

Resolve Action Center warnings

Set up parental controls

Create your first back-up

Assessing what's provided

Your PC was not shipped to you with all of the available safety measures in place. While many measures are enabled by default, which you'll learn about later, some require intervention from you.

Here's an example. If you have grandchildren who use your computer, they could possibly access or delete your personal data, download harmful content, install applications or change settings that will affect the entire computer – all very easily. You can solve all of these problems by creating a computer account just for them. In conjunction, every account you create should be password-protected, especially yours. It wouldn't do much good to create accounts and not assign passwords!

Beyond creating user accounts, here are some other ways to protect your PC, which we'll discuss in depth in this chapter:

- System Restore – If enabled, Windows 7 stores 'restore points' on your PC's hard drive. If something goes wrong you can run System Restore, choose one of these points, and revert to a pre-problem date. Since System Restore only deals with 'system data', none of your personal data will be affected (not even your last e-mail).

- Windows Update – If enabled and configured properly, when you are online, Windows 7 will check for security updates automatically and install them. You don't have to do anything and your PC is always updated with the latest security patches and features.

- Windows Firewall – If enabled and configured properly, the firewall will help prevent hackers (people whose job it is to get into your computer and do harm to it) from accessing your PC and data. The firewall blocks most programs from communicating outside the network (or outside your PC). If you want to allow a program to communicate outside your safety zone you can 'allow' a program by adding it to an 'exceptions' list. This is all very easy to do.

- Windows Defender – You don't have to do much to Windows Defender except understand that it offers protection against Internet threats. It's enabled by default and it runs in the background. However, if you ever think your computer has been attacked by an Internet threat (virus, worm, malware, etc.) you can run a manual scan here.

- Action Center Warnings – The Action Center is a talkative application. You can be sure you'll see a pop-up if your anti-virus software is out of date (or not installed), if you don't have the proper security settings configured or if Windows Update or the Firewall is disabled. You'll learn about warnings and what to do about them in this chapter.

- Parental Controls – If you have grandchildren, children or even a forgetful or scatterbrained partner who needs imposed computer limitations, you can apply them using parental controls. With these controls you are in charge of the hours a user can access the computer, which games they can play and what programs they can run (among other things).

- Backup and Restore – This feature lets you perform back-ups and, in the case of a computer failure, restore them (put them back). However, there are other back-up options too, including copying files to a CD or DVD, copying pictures and media to an external hard drive, USB drive or memory card or storing them on an Internet server.

Assessing what's provided (cont.)

10

User accounts and passwords

If every person who accesses your PC has their own standard user account and password, and if every person logs on using that account and then logs off the PC each time they've finished using it, you'll never have to worry about anyone accessing anyone else's personal data. That's because when a user logs on with their own user account, they can only access their own data (and any data other users have specifically elected to share).

Additionally, every user with their own user account is provided with a 'user profile' that tells Windows 7 what desktop background to use, what screensaver and preferences for mouse settings, sounds, and more. Each user also has their own Favorites in Internet Explorer 7 and their own e-mail settings, address books and personal folders. User accounts help everyone who accesses the computer to keep their personal data, well, personal.

Also, by creating standard accounts for users (yes, even yourself) instead of administrator accounts, you can keep the computer safe by requiring administrator credentials to make system-wide changes like installing applications, changing security settings and accessing every file on the PC. Even if you are the only person who accesses your PC, you should still create a standard account for yourself and use it. If someone does break into your home or come by unexpectedly, they won't be able to use your PC without your standard account password. And, if they try to do something that may harm the PC, they'll also have to know your administrator credentials and administrator password. That being the case, hackers won't be able to get in as easily either.

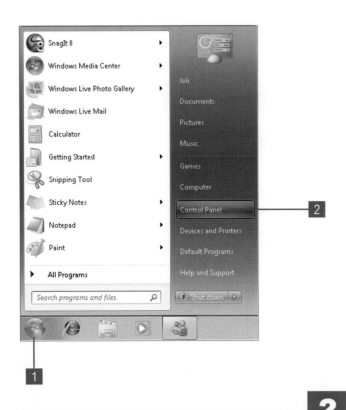

Add a new user account

1 Click Start.

2 Click Control Panel.

3 Click Add or remove user accounts.

Did you know?

Control Panel has different views. If you don't see what's shown here, click the View by button. You can choose from Category (the default), Large icons and Small icons.

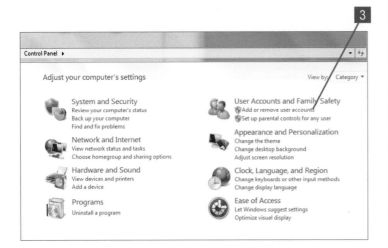

10

User accounts and passwords (cont.)

4 Click Create a new account.

5 Type a new account name. This should be the user's name. If you are creating a new standard account for yourself, stop. Read the section The administrator account dilemma, right, before continuing. These steps are for creating an account for someone else, like a child, grandchild or partner.

6 Verify Standard user is selected.

7 Click Create Account.

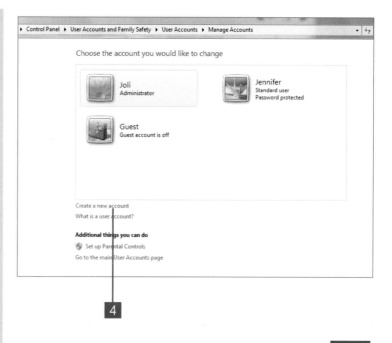

Important

If your administrator account is not password protected, or if you see any other accounts that are not password protected, work through the task on page 224, Require passwords, to apply them.

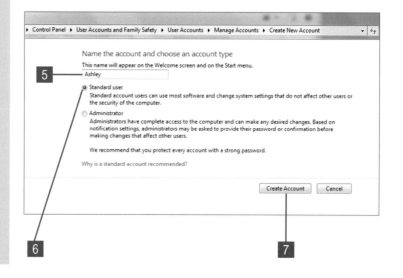

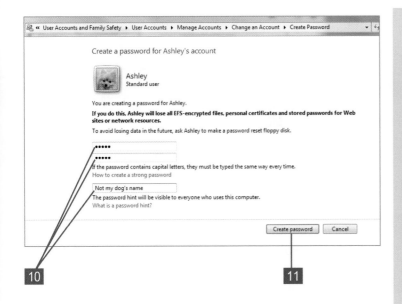

10

11

---

8 Click the new account.

9 Click Create a password.

10 Type the new password, type it again to confirm it and type a password hint.

11 Click Create password.

12 Click the X in the top right-hand corner to close the window.

For your information

You can also click Change the picture, Change the account name, Remove the password, and other options to further personalise the account.

The administrator account dilemma

It's very likely you're logging on to your PC using an administrator account. That's because when you set up Windows 7, it made you create an administrator account! Nowhere did it tell you to create a standard account later or otherwise inform you of the importance of it. That said, all of your personal data, preferences, e-mail settings and other configurations are probably applied to an administrator account, which causes several problems when moving to a standard account.

10

User accounts and passwords (cont.)

Find out if you're logging on using an administrator account

1. Click Start.

2. Click Control Panel.

3. Click Add or remove user accounts.

4. If the account you log on with says Administrator, as shown here, you're using an administrator account.

Move from an administrator to a standard account

1. Click Start.

2. Click Control Panel.

3. Click Add or remove user accounts.

4. Click Create new account.

5. Type Admin for the account name. Select Administrator.

6. Click Create Account.

7. Click the new Admin account.

As stated, you should be using a standard account exclusively. Unfortunately, if you simply create a new standard account for yourself, when you log on to the PC using your new account, it's like logging on to the PC for the first time. You have to reconfigure your Desktop background, screensaver, applications, e-mail, Internet Favorites and find some way to move or copy your personal folders to the new account. Although it's not impossible, it is a royal pain. That being the case, if you really want to switch from an administrator account to a standard one, you'll have to work through the steps in the following task.

Important

Only work through this task if you've read The administrator account dilemma and are positive you currently log on using an administrator account.

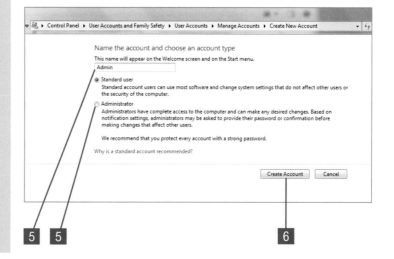

Make changes to Joli's account

Change the account name

Create a password ———————————— 8

Change the picture

Set up Parental Controls

Change the account type ———————————— 15

Delete the account

Manage another account

For your information

When viewing all user accounts on the PC, make note of any that are not password protected. Apply passwords to those accounts as detailed in the next task.

Important

Write down your user name and password and keep it in a safe place.

8 Click Create a password.

9 Type the new password, type it again to confirm it, and type a password hint. It's best to create a password that contains upper- and lower-case letters and a few numbers. Write the password down and keep it somewhere out of sight and safe. Each time you need to make a system-wide change, you'll need to input Admin and the password to obtain access.

10 Click Create password. (Note that you can also click Change the picture, Change the account name, Remove the password, and other options to further personalise the account.)

11 Click the back arrow as needed to return to the window that contains the list of user accounts.

12 Click your old administrator account, not the new Admin account.

13 In the resulting window, click Change the account type.

14 Click Standard user.

15 Click Change the account type.

16 Click Start.

17 Click the right arrow.

10

User accounts and passwords (cont.)

18 Click Log off.

19 Log back in using your new standard account (which is your old user name and credentials).

Require passwords

1 Click Start.

2 Click Control Panel.

3 Click Add or remove user accounts.

4 Click the user account to apply a password to.

5 Click Create a password.

6 Type the new password, type it again to confirm it, and type a password hint. It's best to create a password that contains upper- and lower-case letters and a few numbers. Write the password down and keep it somewhere out of sight and safe.

7 Click Create password. (Note that you can also click Change the picture, Change the account name, Remove the password, and other options to further personalise the account.)

8 Click the X in the top right of the window to close it.

For your information

When logged on as a standard user, and when you need to make a change to the system that affects everyone, you will either be prompted to insert the Admin password or simply be told you are not allowed to make this change. If prompted that you simply don't have access, you'll have to log off and log back on as an Admin to complete the change. It's much more likely you'll be prompted to input the Admin password. What you see depends on how other security features are configured. Whatever happens though, the security enhancement you get by using a standard account far outweighs the nuisance of the occasional security message.

You learned a little about System Restore, Windows Update, Windows Firewall and Windows Defender in the Introduction. Now it's time to take a look at each of these more closely, and to verify they are set up properly and running as they should be.

System Restore

System Restore lets you restore your computer to an earlier time without affecting your personal files, including documents, spreadsheets, e-mail and photos. You'll only use System Restore if and when you install a program or driver that ultimately produces error messages or causes problems for the computer and uninstalling the problematic application or driver doesn't resolve the issue.

System Restore, by default, regularly creates and saves restore points that contain information about registry settings and deep-down system information that Windows uses to work properly. Because System Restore works only with its own system files, it can't recover a lost personal file, e-mail or picture. In the same vein, it will not affect this data either.

Protecting your PC

Did you know?

System Restore can't be enabled unless the computer has at least 300 MB of free space on the hard disk or if the disk is smaller than 1 GB.

10

Protecting your PC (cont.)

Use System Restore

1 Click Start.

2 In the Search box, type System Restore.

3 Click System Restore under the Programs results.

4 Read the information and click Next.

5 Verify that restore points are available, and select a restore point. You'll want to select a point that is just prior to the problem occurring.

6 Click Next.

7 Click Finish to run System Restore, otherwise click Cancel.

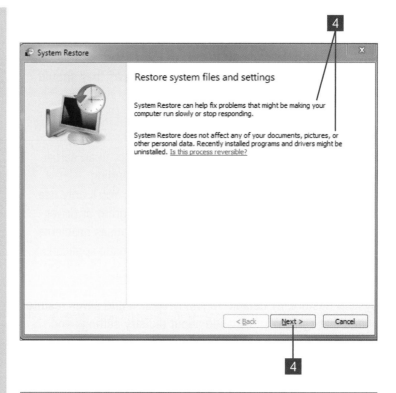

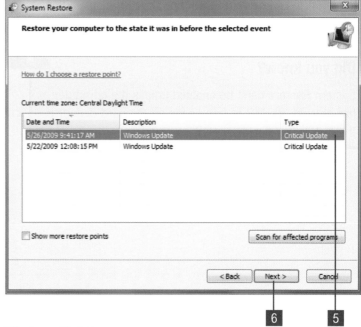

Windows Update

It's very important to configure Windows Update to get and install updates automatically. This is the easiest way to ensure your computer is as up to date as possible, at least as far as patching security flaws Microsoft uncovers, having access to the latest features and obtaining updates to the operating system itself are concerned. I propose you verify that the recommended settings are enabled as detailed here, and occasionally check for optional updates manually.

When Windows Update is configured as recommended in the task here, updates will be downloaded automatically when you are online (on the Internet), installed and, if necessary, your computer will be rebooted automatically. You can configure the time of day you want this to happen.

Note: The Windows Help and Support Center offers pages upon pages of information regarding Windows Update, including how to remove them or select updates when more than one is available. I think the above paragraphs state all you need to know as an average 50+ computer user, and you need not worry about anything else regarding Windows Update.

Configure Windows Update

1 Click Start.

2 Click Control Panel.

3 Click System and Security.

4 Click Windows Update.

10

Protecting your PC (cont.)

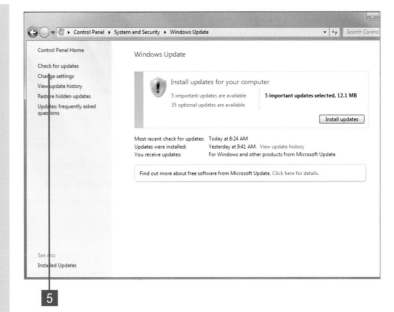

5 You may see that Windows is up to date, or you may see that there are available updates. Anything else means that Windows Update is not configured using recommended settings. Whatever the case, click Change settings.

6 Verify the settings are configured to Install updates automatically (recommended) as shown here. (If you desire, you can choose another setting, but I don't recommend it.)

7 Notice the default time of 3:00 a.m. You can change this to a time when your PC is connected to the Internet but is not being used. This is not necessary, actually, if the computer is not online at 3:00 a.m., it will check for updates the next time it is.

8 Verify the items ticked here are ticked on your PC.

9 Make changes if needed, and click OK.

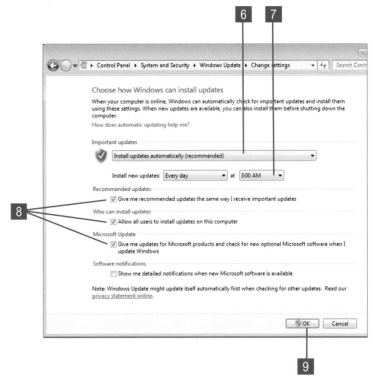

If you see that optional components are available (or any other updates for that matter), you can view and install them by clicking Install updates. If prompted, select the items to update and click OK. You do not have to install optional updates.

For your information

You may have to restart the computer after installing the updates.

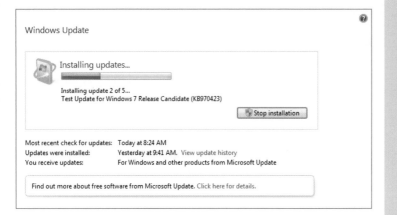

Windows Update

Installing updates...

Installing update 2 of 5...
Test Update for Windows 7 Release Candidate (KB970423)

Stop installation

Most recent check for updates: Today at 8:24 AM
Updates were installed: Yesterday at 9:41 AM. View update history
You receive updates: For Windows and other products from Microsoft Update

Find out more about free software from Microsoft Update. Click here for details.

For your information

To turn off Windows Update, which we do not suggest or recommend, click View options. There, you will have the option to disable this feature.

Windows security features

There are two more security features to explore: Windows Firewall and Windows Defender. There isn't much you need to do with these features except to make sure they are both enabled and are protecting your PC. By default, both are enabled.

Windows Firewall is a software program that checks the data that comes from the Internet (or a local network) and then decides whether it's good data or bad. If it deems the data harmless, it will allow it to come through the firewall; if not, it's blocked. You have to have a firewall to keep hackers from getting access to your PC, and to help prevent your computer from sending out malicious code if it is ever attacked by a virus or worm.

Protecting your PC (cont.)

Sometimes the firewall will block programs you want to use, including but not limited to:

- Windows Live Messenger
- Microsoft Office Outlook
- Remote Assistance
- Windows Media Player
- Wireless Portable Devices.

These and others are blocked by default, and the first time you try to use them you'll be prompted to unblock them. There is reasoning behind this, and it has to do with protecting you from Internet ills. A hacker may try to come through the Internet to your PC using an application you don't normally use, like Remote Assistance. It can't come through unless you 'allow' it to. (When unblocking a program you can ask that you not be prompted again regarding that particular application.)

Windows Defender protects your PC against malicious and unwanted software. Generally this is a type of data called spyware, malware or adware. Spyware can install itself on your PC without your knowledge and can wreak havoc by causing these types of problems:

- Adding toolbars to Internet Explorer.
- Changing Internet Explorer's Home page.
- Taking you to websites you do not want to visit.
- Showing pop-up advertisements.
- Causing the computer to perform slowly.

Windows Defender helps protect this type of data from getting onto your PC, and thus limits infection on PCs.

It's up to you to make sure that the Firewall and Windows Defender are running and configured properly. That's what you'll do in the next two tasks. Additionally, you'll have the option of changing a few of the parameters, such as when scans are completed and what happens when potentially dangerous data is detected.

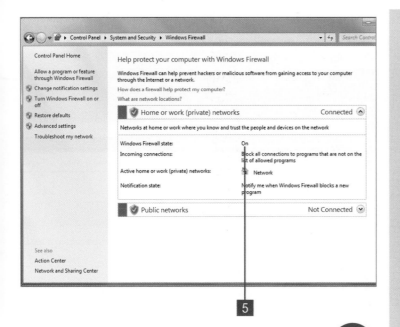

5

For your information

To manually allow a program or a feature through the firewall, click Allow a program or feature through Windows Firewall. Select the feature or program to allow and click OK. You can manually enable exceptions here or simply wait until you're prompted when trying to use the application.

Use Windows Firewall

1 Click Start.

2 Click Control Panel.

3 Click System and Security.

4 Under Windows Firewall, click Check firewall status.

5 Verify the firewall is On. If it is, you are finished and can close the window. If not, select Turn Windows Firewall on or off.

6 Select Turn on Windows Firewall and accept the default settings. Click OK.

7 Click OK.

10

Protecting your PC (cont.)

Use Windows Defender

1 Click Start.

2 In the Search window, type Windows Defender.

3 Under the results for Control Panel, click Windows Defender.

4 Hopefully, you'll see that no unwanted or harmful software has been detected. If it has (and this is highly unlikey), you'll be prompted regarding what to do next. Click Tools.

5 Click Options.

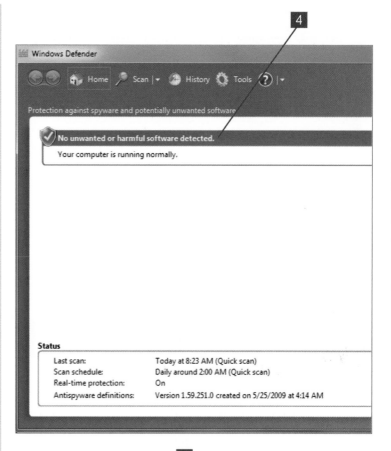

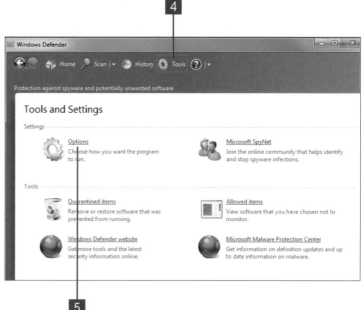

Check out the additional options in Windows Defender in addition to Automatic scanning. Click each option to view it.

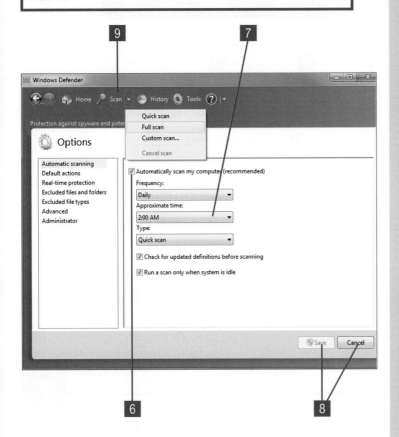

6 Verify that Automatic scanning is enabled.

7 If desired, change the approximate time of the scan. It's best to leave the other defaults as is.

8 Click Save if you've made changes, or Cancel if not.

9 Click the arrow next to Scan (not the Scan icon). Note that you can manually perform a Quick scan or a Full scan. Do this if you think the computer has been infected.

Resolving Action Center warnings

Last but not least, you need to occasionally visit the Action Center to see if any warnings exist. If you see anything in red, the problem needs to be resolved. In the example overleaf, a problem exists; there's no virus protection.

10

Protecting your PC (cont.)

Resolve Action Center warnings

1. Locate the Action Center icon in the Notification area of the Taskbar.

2. Click it, and click Open Action Center.

3. If there's anything in red (or yellow), read about the problem. If there's an option to resolve it, click it. Here you can see Find an antivirus program online (Important).

4. Note the resolution and perform the task.

Did you know?

To change how often you're notified about changes made to your computer, click Change User Account Control settings in the Action Center window.

For your information

To learn more about the amount of RAM, type of processor, and graphics card installed in your PC, click View performance information in the Action Center window.

There are two other things you can do to protect your family and data. First, protect the children and grandchildren with parental controls. Parental controls isn't a cure-all, but it does help. You still have to find a way to protect your family from Internet bad guys when they're away from home, but at least while they're under your roof you can look after them. Second, learn how to create back-ups of your data and settings. Although it's unlikely something will happen in the immediate future that is so bad it would destroy your PC and all of your data, it could happen (and it does). It's best to be prepared.

Parental controls

As noted earlier, parental controls can be applied to children, grandchildren, guests and even partners. You can configure parental controls to set limits on when a person can use the computer (and for how long), what games they can play, what websites they can visit and what programs they can run. Once you've configured parental controls, you can review 'activity reports' that let you see what that person has been doing with their computer time. You can also view what content has been blocked, which will allow you to see how far the user has been testing the limits of the controls you've set.

Important

You can only apply parental controls to users with a Standard user account. Additionally, all other user accounts should have passwords so that the standard user cannot log on with another account when they are not allowed on the PC.

With parental controls, there are options to set time limits, games and access to programs. There is also an option to enable web filtering and activity reporting using an additional service you purchase and/or configure.

Protecting your family and your data

10

Protecting your family and your data (cont.)

Set up parental controls

1. Click Start.

2. Click Control Panel.

3. Under User Accounts and Family Safety, click Set up parental controls for any user.

4. Click the standard user account for which you want to set parental controls. It's OK if this is the only account without a password, but it is still suggested one is applied.

5. Under Parental Controls, click On.

6. Click Time limits.

7. Click and drag to set times to block and allow. Blue is blocked.

8. Click OK.

9. Click Back to the page shown for Step 5 and click Games.

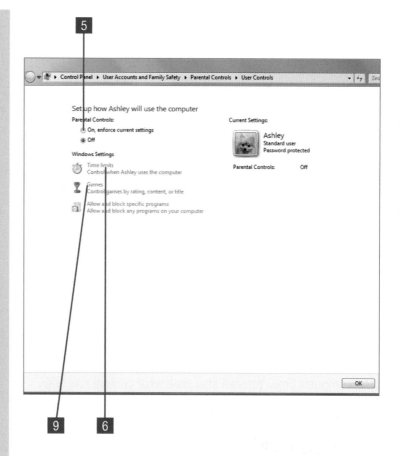

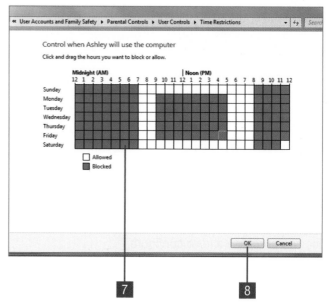

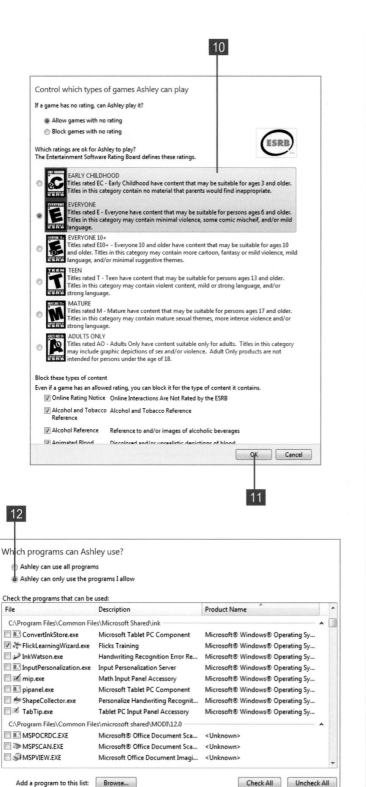

10 Click Yes to allow games to be played, or No to disallow it. If you click Yes:

a. Click Set Game Ratings and select an age group from the resulting list.

b. Click to block specific types of content.

c. Click OK.

11 Click OK to close Game Controls.

12 Click Back as in Step 9, then Allow and block specific programs. If the user can access all programs, select <user name> can use all programs. Otherwise, choose <user name> can only use the programs I allow. For the latter, select and deselect programs the user can run. Click OK.

10

Protecting your family and your data (cont.)

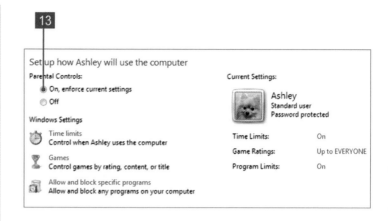

13

13 Notice in the Parental Controls window you can verify the settings.

14 Click OK.

15 Click the X in the top right-hand corner to close the Parental Controls window.

Create your first back-up

1 Click Start.

2 Click Control Panel.

3 Click Back up your computer. (It's under System and Security.)

4 Click Set up backup.

Backing up data

Windows 7 comes with a back-up program you can use to back up your personal data. The back-up program is called Backup and Restore.

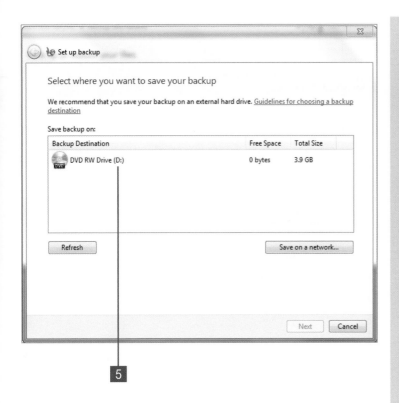

5 Choose a place to save your back-up. Since back-ups can be large, consider a USB drive, external hard drive or DVD. You can also choose a network location. For the first back-up, if possible select a location that has several GBs of space (like an external hard drive or network location), just to be safe.

For your information

To choose a network location, such as another computer on your home network, click Save on a network... Locate the folder and input credentials to access the computer (your administrator name and password will do). Click OK to apply the changes.

Did you know?

You can't create a back-up on the hard disk of the computer you are backing up.

10

Protecting your family and your data (cont.)

6 Click Next. (If prompted for any other information, such as a hard drive partition, to insert a blank DVD or insert a USB drive, do so.)

7 Select what to back up. First timers should select Let Windows choose (recommended). Click Next.

8 Note the time and date for the back-ups to occur. In this case, it's every Sunday at 7:00 p.m. If you want to, click Change settings below Schedule and choose settings for how often, what day, and what time future back-ups should occur.

9 Click Save settings and start back-up.

10 Follow the same procedure to restore data from a back-up if and when necessary.

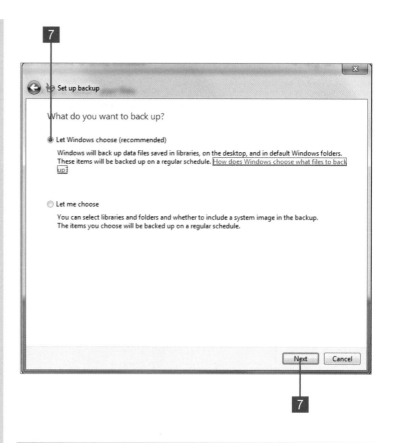

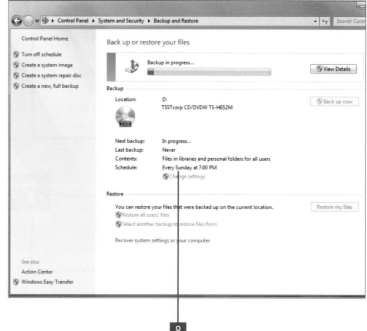

Jargon buster

Adware – Internet advertisements (which are also applications) that often include additional code that can be used to track a user's personal information and pass it on to third parties, without the user's authorisation or knowledge.

Internet server – a computer that stores data off site. Hotmail offers Internet servers to hold e-mail and data, so that you do not have to store it on your PC. Internet servers allow you to access information from any computer that can access the Internet.

Virus – a self-replicating program that infects computers with intent to do harm. Viruses often come in the form of an attachment in an e-mail.

Worm – a self-replicating program that infects computers with intent to do harm. However, unlike a virus, it does not need to attach itself to a running program.

10

Media applications

Introduction

Windows 7 comes with several media applications, including Windows Media Player, Windows Media Center and Windows DVD Maker. You've probably also downloaded Windows Live Essentials, including programs you'll need to round out your media requirements including (but not limited to) Windows Live Photo Gallery. (If you haven't downloaded Windows Live Essentials, refer to Chapter 1 for more information on how to do that.)

You can use these applications to watch DVDs, watch, pause and record live TV, listen to and download music, movies and video, create your own movies from your own video footage, and manage your digital pictures. In this chapter you'll learn just enough about many of these applications to get started. There's a lot more to them than what you'll see here though, so you'll want to experiment on your own. Remember, you can't hurt anything; and even if you did, you could use System Restore to fix it!

What you'll do

Explore Windows Media Player

Listen to sample music in Media Player

Rip your CD collection in Media Player

Burn a CD in Media Player

Explore the Photo Gallery interface

Add a folder to Windows Photo Gallery

Personalise Photo Gallery

Import pictures from a digital camera, media card or USB drive (and even an iPhone)

Fix pictures

Add picture information (tagging)

E-mail pictures

Watch a DVD in Media Center

Create a professional DVD with Windows DVD Maker (parts I and II)

Watch live TV in Media Center

Record a TV show or series in Media Center

Using Windows Media Player

Windows Media Player offers all you'll need to manage your music library, get music online and copy the CDs from your own music collection to your PC. You can also use it to burn music CDs you can listen to in your car, share music using your local network, and more.

Windows Media Player stands apart from other applications because it's used to acquire, play, share and listen to music. You can also work with video and pictures, but for the most part, you'll use Media Player for music management. That said, if you've never used a music application on a PC or mobile device, there are a few things you'll need to know beforehand. So, before we get started, let's review some terms you'll see throughout this part of the chapter:

- Playlist – a group of songs that you can save and then listen to as a group, burn to a CD, copy to a portable music player, and more.

- Rip – a term used to describe the process of copying files from a physical CD to your hard drive, and thus your music library.

- Burn – a term used to describe the process of copying music from a computer to a CD or DVD. Generally music is burned to a CD, since CDs can be played in cars and generic CD players, and videos are burned to DVDs since they require much more space and can be played on DVD players.

If you've never used Windows Media Player, the first time you open it you'll have to work though a wizard to tell Windows Media Player how you want it to perform. You'll have two options: Express or Custom. If you're new to Media Player it's OK to select Express and accept the defaults. You can always change any options you decide you don't like after you've worked with it for a while.

After completing set-up, you'll probably see exactly what's shown right, including the sample music offered. You'll see familiar attributes, like the Back and Forward buttons, and menus. You'll also see tab titles: Play, Burn and Sync, on the right side of the Menu bar. Look deeper and you'll also see Media Guide (bottom left).

On the left pane you can access playlists you can create and everything in your music library. You can sort by artist, album and genre, by default, but you can also right-click Music to access the command Customize Navigation Pane where you can then add additional categories like year, rating, composer, and more. To play any song, double-click it.

As with other applications native to Windows 7, there are options for changing the layout and view, and a Search box. Let's look at a few of these options now.

Choosing a category and the resulting view

So as not to get lost, we'll take this a step at a time. Overleaf you'll see the Library button, top left. If you click the arrow to the right of this button, you can navigate to all of the media on your PC from the drop-down list shown, including music, videos, pictures, recorded TV and other media, including radio stations you like.

The Music view is the default, because almost everyone will use Media Player for music and something else for other media. You'll probably prefer to work with photos in Windows Live Photo Gallery, for instance, and television in Media Center.

Using Windows Media Player (cont.)

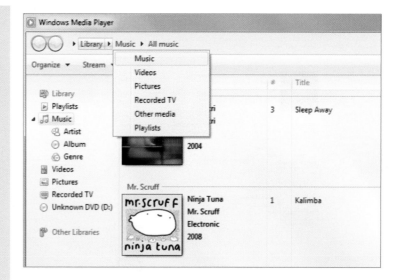

When you make a selection from the Library menu options above, what you see in the left pane will change. By default, Music is selected. However, here's what happens when you select Pictures.

Double-click All pictures to see the pictures on your PC (see right). As you can imagine, selecting other categories offers similar results.

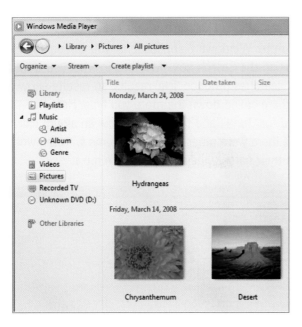

For your information

Show the Menu bar to have access to familiar menus like File, View, Play, Tools and Help.

Did you know?

You can show the Menu bar only when you need it by clicking the Alt key on the keyboard.

Show the Menu bar

The Organize button offers several options you'll want to explore, including Customize navigation pane, Layout and Options. If you select an item in the list that has an arrow by it, click it to see additional options. Here, Layout is selected, and I've highlighted Show menu bar. I think it's best to show the Menu bar and, if you agree, click it.

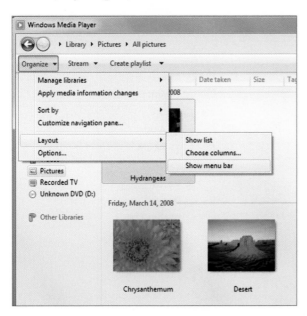

Using Windows Media Player (cont.)

Explore Windows Media Player

1. Open Windows Media Player.

2. If you are not in the Music library, click the arrow next to the Library button and select Music, or click Music in the Navigation pane.

Search

As with other Windows 7 applications, you can search for media using the Search box. Just type in what you want to find. Its searches produce 'live' results, so results show as you type and are culled down the more you type. Here I've searched for 'Tuna', and the results show an album called Ninja Tuna. (If there were other songs or albums with the word 'tuna' in their names, they'd appear here too.)

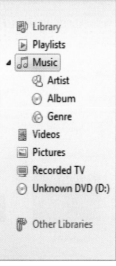

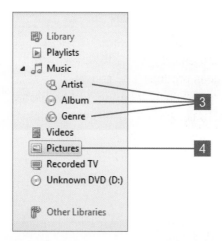

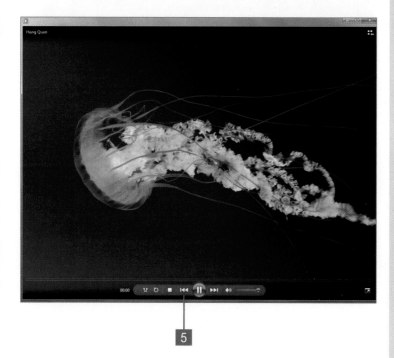

5

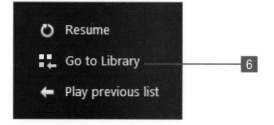

6

3 In the Navigation pane, select Artist, then Album, then Songs, and then Genre to see the differing views. (Return to Music when finished.)

4 From the Navigation Pane, select Pictures. You can also click the arrow next to the Library button to access Pictures.

5 Double-click the first image. It will appear in full-screen mode and a slide show of the images in this folder will begin. (Notice the controls at the bottom of the slide show. You can use these controls to move through the media that's playing.)

6 When the slide show has finished, click Go to Library.

Using Windows Media Player (cont.)

9

7 Click Recorded TV.

8 Double-click the video to play it.

9 Position your mouse at the bottom of the screen to show the controls.

10 Continue experimenting as desired.

Important

!

If Windows Media Player seems to disappear, check your Taskbar. To bring it back to the Desktop, click the Media Player button.

Now that you're somewhat familiar with the Media Player interface, let's play some music. To play any music track (or view any picture, watch any video or view other media), simply navigate to it and double-click it.

For your information

You can select a song in the album list to play it, or click Play to play the entire album.

6

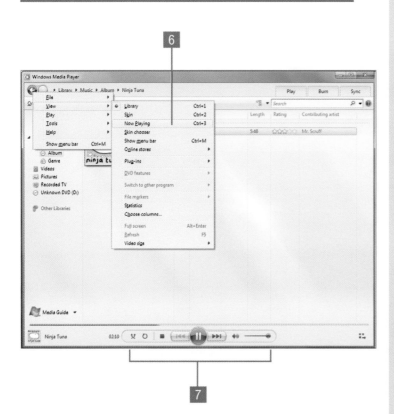

7

Playing media

11

Listen to sample music in Media Player

1 Open Media Player.

2 If necessary, in the Navigation pane, click Music.

3 Click Album.

4 Double-click any album to play it.

5 Double-click the album again or click the Play button. You'll see the progress of the album at the bottom of the page.

6 Click View, and click Now Playing. If you can't see the View menu shown here, click Ctrl+M on the keyboard or click the Alt key.

7 Note the controls at the bottom of the interface. From left to right: Shuffle (to play songs in random order), Repeat, Stop, Previous, Play/Pause, Next, Mute, and a volume slider. Use these controls to manage the song and to move from one song to the next.

Media applications 251

Playing media (cont.)

8 Click Switch to Library to return to the Library. The Switch to Library button is in the upper right-hand corner; you have to hover your mouse over it to show it.

9 Continue experimenting with the controls until you are comfortable playing music.

Did you know?

To the right of the controls is an option to View full screen. While in full screen mode, the option changes to exit the mode.

To rip means to copy in media-speak. When you rip a CD, you copy the CD to your PC's hard drive. If you have a large CD collection, this could take some time, but it will ultimately be worth it. Once music is on your PC, you can listen to it in Media Player, burn compilations of music to other CDs and even put the music on a portable music player, like a Zune.

To rip a CD, simply put the CD in the CD drive, close any pop-up boxes and, in Media Player, click the Rip CD button. During the copy process, you can watch the progress of the rip. By default, music will be saved in your Music folder.

Rip your CD collection in Media Player

1 Insert the CD to copy into the CD drive.

2 If any pop-up boxes appear, click the X to close out of them. This step isn't actually necessary, as you can select Rip CD in Windows Media Player from the dialogue box shown here, but I'd like to introduce ripping from Media Player, not from a dialogue box, so that you can access all available options.

3 Deselect any songs you do not want to copy to your PC. (All songs are selected by default.)

4 In Windows Media Player, click the Rip CD button.

5 The ripped music will now appear in your music library in various places including Artist, Album and Genre.

Did you know?

You can deselect songs during the rip process if you decide you don't want them to be copied.

Burning a CD

There are two ways to take music with you when you are on the road or on the go. You can copy the music to a portable device, like a mobile phone, Zune or other music player (and keep it synchronised using Media Player), or you can create your own CDs, choosing the songs to copy and placing them on the CD in the desired order. CDs you create can be played in car stereos and portable CD players, as well as lots of other CD devices. A typical CD can hold about 80 minutes of music, but don't worry, Media Player will keep track of the songs you select and will let you know when you're running out of space on the CD you're creating.

The Burn tab can assist you in creating a CD. 'Burn' is media-speak for copying music from your PC to a CD. Clicking Burn brings up the List pane, where Media Player will tell you to insert a blank CD if one is not in the drive already, and allow you to drag and drop songs into the List pane to create a burn list. As music is added, the progress bar at the top of the List pane shows how much available space you've used.

For your information

Once you've added music to the List pane, the Start Burn button becomes active.

Did you know?

You can right-click any song in the Burn list to access additional options, including the option to delete the song from the list (not the PC), or to move up or move down in the list order.

Burn a CD in Media Player

1 Open Media Player.

2 Click the Burn tab.

3 Insert a blank recordable CD into the CD drive.

4 Under Library, click Music.

5 Click any song title to add, and drag it to the List pane.

6 Drop the song in the List pane to add it to the burn list. Continue as desired.

7 Look at the slider in the List pane to verify there is room left on the CD. Continue to add songs until the CD is full or until desired.

8 When you've added the songs you want, click Start Burn.

For your information

You have to have a recordable CD drive installed to burn your own CDs.

Did you know?

Click the blue question mark next to the Search box for more information on how to use Windows Media Player.

For your information

You do not need to fill the entire CD with songs if you don't want to.

Windows Live Photo Gallery

Windows Live Photo Gallery may be all you need to manage, manipulate, view and share your digital photos. Before you install additional software, including software that was included on the CD that shipped with your digital camera or printer, try this program. It's not included with Windows 7 though; it requires you download and install it. That's covered in Chapter 1, so if you haven't done that yet, return there to learn how. Windows Live Photo Gallery requires no additional hardware, although you may want to install a printer or scanner. Note that you can also manage videos with Windows Live Photo Gallery, but Windows Media Center is better for that, which we'll talk about later in this chapter.

The Photo Gallery interface

Windows Live Photo Gallery has two default panes and each offers specific functionality. When you open Windows Live Photo Gallery, the pane to the left is the Navigation pane, where you'll select the folder or subfolder that contains the pictures you want to view, manage, edit or share. The Thumbnail pane (or View pane) is on the right, and this is where you preview the pictures in the folder selected in the View pane.

The first time you open Windows Live Photo Gallery you'll be prompted to associate your picture files with it. For now, click Yes, but do not select Don't show me this again for these file types. Later, once you're sure you want to use this program for managing your digital pictures, select it to stop showing the message.

When you double-click a picture in the Thumbnail pane, it opens in a new pane where you can then edit, share, add tags and perform other image-related tasks. Note that when you double-click an image, the View pane disappears and a new pane appears on the right. From that new pane, called the Info pane, you can rate the image and add tags easily.

At the bottom of the Info pane are the navigational controls. Here you can move from picture to picture in the current folder, rotate pictures, delete pictures and even zoom in, among other things.

There are other navigational controls, including a toggle switch to move from the image's actual size to fit to screen, arrows for Previous (to move to the previous picture in the folder), Play Slide Show (to play a slide show of the folder's pictures), Next (to move to the next picture in the folder), Rotate Counterclockwise, Rotate Clockwise, and Delete.

Jargon buster

JPG (JPEG), TIF, PNG, WDP, BMP, ICO – Each of these is a 'file name extension', and describes a type of image file. JPG is almost always the default picture format used with digital cameras for sending in e-mail, and for storing digital images.

Did you know?

You can perform hundreds of tasks in Windows Photo Gallery, including fixing red-eye, adjusting the colour, cropping a photo, publishing images to an online photo album, e-mailing photos, printing or ordering prints online, making a movie, burning a DVD, and more.

Windows Live Photo Gallery (cont.)

Did you know?

The next time you want to open Windows Live Photo Gallery, look on the Start menu; it just might be there!

Explore the Photo Gallery interface

1 Click Start.

2 Click All programs.

3 Click Windows Live and click Windows Live Photo Gallery.

4 Click All photos and videos in the Navigation pane on the left side.

5 Locate the navigational controls. Use the zoom slider to increase or decrease the size of the thumbnails.

6 Click any other folder to see the pictures inside it. You may only have the Sample Pictures folder.

For your information

Click the arrow next to any folder to expand it, if necessary, to see the images in the folder.

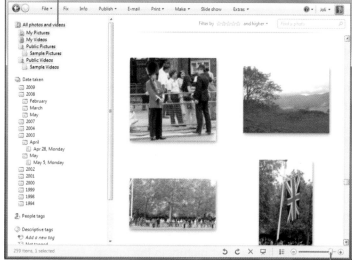

7 Hover the mouse over any small thumbnail in the Thumbnail pane to see a larger thumbnail.

8 Double-click any picture in any folder.

9 Click the F12 key on the keyboard to start a slide show of the pictures. Click the Esc key to stop and return to Windows Live Photo Gallery.

10 Right-click any image.

11 Click Properties.

12 Note the Details tab and the picture details. You can view the picture size and the camera used to take the picture, among other things. Click OK.

13 Double-click any picture.

14 Click Back to Gallery.

15 If desired, click File, and click Exit to close Photo Gallery, or simply leave it open for the next task.

Windows Live Photo Gallery (cont.)

Add a folder to Windows Photo Gallery

1 If you don't want to move pictures and videos from folders you've created outside of the default Pictures, Public Pictures, Videos, or Public Videos folder, you'll need to perform the steps here to tell Windows Live Photo Gallery where they are. To start, open Windows Live Photo Gallery.

2 Click File.

3 Click Include a folder in the gallery...

Adding folders to Windows Photo Gallery

Windows 7 takes care of storing your digital files and offers several folders for doing so, including Pictures, Public Pictures, Videos, and Public Videos, and Windows Live Photo Gallery lets you easily manage the data you put inside these folders in a single interface. However, Windows Live Photo Gallery only looks in the *default folders* for media. That means if you create a folder on your Desktop called Digital Photos from my 2009 Trip to Italy, or if you store pictures on a networked computer or external drive, the photos and videos in those folders won't appear in Photo Gallery by default. So, if you've stored pictures and videos in folders other than Pictures, Videos, Public Pictures, and Public Videos, you have two options. You can either move the photos to those folders or tell Windows Live Photo Gallery you want it to watch those folders for media.

For your information

Remember, when moving data, right-click while dragging from one folder to another, and then select Move when you're ready to drop the data. Alternatively, you can select the data to move, right-click, choose Cut, and then right-click, and choose Paste to move it to the correct folder.

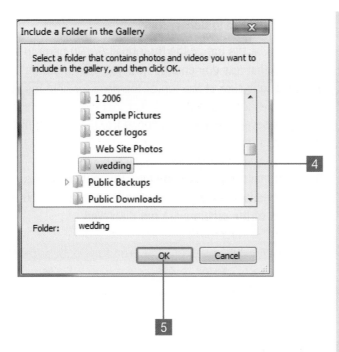

4 Expand the 'trees' to locate the folder to add. To do this, click the down arrow by the desired option. (Note that you can resize this window by dragging from the bottom right corner.) Here I've browsed to a folder located on my computer network, to a computer named Windows Vista, to a public folder.

5 Click OK.

6 Click OK again, when prompted.

7 Once added, a new folder will appear in the View pane.

Windows Live Photo Gallery (cont.)

Changing the Photo Gallery View

Right-click at the top of the thumbnail (View) pane to access the menu that lets you change how you view pictures by default. Right-click at the top of the pane for best results.

There are several options to choose from, including but not limited to:

- Thumbnails – The default style. This option shows thumbnails you can resize using the zoom tool, but the names of the pictures are not displayed.

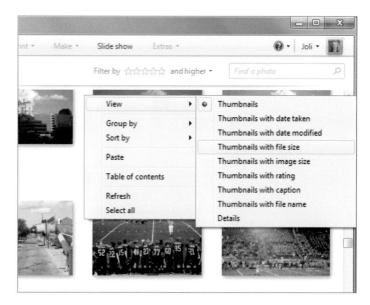

- Thumbnails with date taken – This view is very similar to Thumbnails, but underneath there's a new line of text that shows when the picture was taken.

- Details – This view offers the most information. This view shows a picture's name, date modified, size, dimensions (resolution), rating and caption next to each image thumbnail.

You can also automatically arrange images in the View pane from the Arrange by auto option. As you can see here, you can arrange the thumbnails by name, date or rating, among others.

Personalise Photo Gallery

1 Open Windows Live Photo Gallery.

2 From the View pane, select All photos and videos

3 Right-click an empty area of the View pane, click View, and click Thumbnails with date taken (as shown on previous page). (Note the other options.) The result is shown here.

4 Click the View Details/View Thumbnails button at the bottom of the interface. Note that this changes the view. Click it again to return to the previous view.

5 Continue experimenting as desired.

Importing pictures

There are lots of different hardware options for taking digital pictures, including mobile phones, smart phones, digital cameras, webcams and video cameras. And there are even more ways to store and carry pictures with you, including USB drives, music players and iPods and iPhones. Finally, there are multiple ways to get pictures onto a PC, including using digital cameras, media cards and even scanners. In this section we'll talk about importing pictures from a device to the PC. Remember, the device doesn't necessarily have to be something that takes the pictures; it can be a scanner, USB drive, media card or music player.

When you connect a digital camera, media card or other device that contains pictures, you'll be prompted to select a way to import them. You may see multiple options or only three or four. Whatever the case, choose Import pictures. This will walk you through the Import Pictures and Videos wizard, outlined in the next task.

Import pictures from a digital camera, media card or USB drive (and even an iPhone)

1 Connect the device. If applicable, turn it on. (If this is the first time you have connected the device, you may have to wait while the driver installs. This is almost always automatic.)

2 If prompted, choose Import pictures and videos using Windows Live Photo Gallery.

For your information

If nothing happens when you connect your camera, media card or other hardware, click File and then click Import from a camera or scanner...

3 Click Import all new items now, and type a descriptive name for the group of pictures you're importing.

4 Click Import.

5 If desired, click Erase after importing. This will cause Windows 7 to erase the images from the device after the import is complete and only appears during the import process.

6 Windows Live Photo Gallery will open, and you can view the pictures.

For your information

After you've had a bit of experience importing pictures as a group, as detailed here, you can try your hand at organising them prior to uploading.

Importing pictures (cont.)

Windows 7 won't recognise all devices, but it does a pretty good job. In fact, it will import pictures from many kinds of mobile phones, including the iPhone. However, on the slim chance your device isn't immediately recognised, in Windows Live Photo Gallery, you can click File, and click Import from a camera or scanner... and you'll be given access to additional devices attached to your PC, even scanners.

With pictures now on your PC and available in Windows Photo Gallery, your next step is to perform some editing. As noted earlier, Photo Gallery offers some editing options, including the ability to correct brightness and contrast, colour temperature, tint and saturation, as well as crop images and fix red eye. You may find, after a bit of time with Photo Gallery though, that you need more editing options. If that turns out to be the case, consider Photoshop Elements. It's a great program for beginners and offers all you'll probably ever need.

To begin editing a picture, first double-click it. From the Menu bar, click Fix. In the new pane that appears, choose from the following:

- Auto adjust – This tool automatically assesses the image and alters it, which most of the time results in a better image. However, there's always the Undo button, and you'll probably use it on occasion.

- Adjust exposure – This tool offers slider controls for brightness and contrast. You move these sliders to the left and right to adjust as desired.

- Adjust color – This tool offers slider controls to adjust the temperature, tint and saturation of the photo. Temperature runs from blue to yellow, allowing you to change the 'atmosphere' of the image. Tint runs from green to red, and saturation moves from black and white to colour.

- Straighten photo – This tool automatically straightens photos and offers a slider you can use as well.

- Crop photo – Use this tool to remove parts of a picture you don't want.

- Adjust detail – This tool allows you to sharpen the image and reduce 'noise'. This can help bring a fuzzy or blurry picture into focus. You can apply changes automatically or manually.

- Fix red eye – This lets you draw a rectangle around any eye that has a red dot in it, and the red dot is automatically removed.

- Black and white effects – This tool lets you apply effects to the image, to change the 'tone' (colour) of the image.

Editing photos (cont.)

Fix pictures

1 Open Windows Live Photo Gallery.

2 In the View pane, select any folder that contains pictures.

3 Position the zoom slider so you can see several images at once.

4 Double-click a picture to edit. (It's best not to use the sample pictures; they're already optimised.)

5 Click Fix.

6 Click Auto adjust.

7 If you like the result, go to Step 8. If not, click Undo.

8 Adjust exposure should be open; if not, click it to view the options.

9 Move the sliders for Brightness and Contrast. Click Undo to return to the original image settings. You may need to click Undo more than once.

For your information

If you click Fix and don't see the editing options, click it again. It toggles the options on and off.

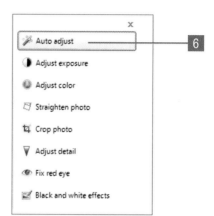

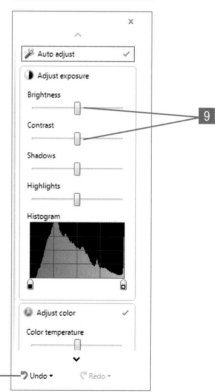

10 Adjust Color should be open, if not click it to view the options.

11 Move the sliders for Color temperature, Tint, and Saturation. Click Undo to return to the original image settings. You may need to click Undo more than once.

12 Click Crop photo. If you can' t see the Crop photo option, either close the open editing options or use the down arrow key to access additional options.

13 Drag the corners of the box to resize it, and drag the entire box to move it around in the picture.

14 If desired, under Proportion, select any option. (Note you can also rotate the frame.)

15 Click Apply or Undo.

16 If there's red eye in the picture, click Fix Red Eye.

17 Drag the mouse over the red part of the eye. When you let go, the red eye in the picture will be removed.

Editing photos (cont.)

18 Click Undo if desired.

19 To save the changes to the original file, i.e. write over the existing file, click Back to Gallery.

20 If you later decide you do not like the changes applied to the picture, double-click it, and choose Revert.

Tags

We've talked a little about tags throughout this chapter. That's because tags can be extremely useful when it comes to organising your photos. You have to apply tags to your photos though, which can be time consuming, but once added, tags can be used to group pictures in useful ways. Some tags are applied automatically when you import pictures from a digital camera, including the date they were uploaded, along with any name you applied to the imported group. While the date is important, tagging a photo (or a group of photos) with a label like wedding, cat, Italy trip or similar names is a great addition.

Although there are several ways to add tags to photos, the easiest, in my opinion, is to create the tag in the View pane, and then select a photo or a group of photos, and drag those photos to the new tag name. The tag will be applied to those photos. Once images are tagged, you can sort them by their tags, as shown here. I created the tag 'Lake', and tagged the photos here with that keyword.

Pictures can have multiple tags too. You might tag a photo as 'Holiday', but also apply tags that name the people in the picture, the city or the country.

Another type of tag is a rating. You can rate pictures from one to five stars, and then filter the pictures as desired. You can add captions too. All of this can be done from the Properties dialogue box, among other places.

Add picture information (tagging)

1 Open Windows Live Photo Gallery.

2 Double-click any picture.

3 Click Info on the Menu bar, note how the Info pane changes to reflect the choice.

Editing photos (cont.)

4 Click Add descriptive tags and type a tag name.

5 Press Enter on the keyboard.

6 To remove the tag (or any other tag), right-click the tag.

7 Click Remove tag.

8 Click Back to Gallery.

9 Scroll down to the bottom of the Navigation pane to Descriptive tags. Click it.

10 Here you can see all of the tags you've created as well as those that were created by Windows Photo Gallery by default. Click any tag to see associated photos.

Did you know?

You can right-click any photo to rename it, delete it, rotate it, resize it, and more.

Did you know?

You can also hover the mouse over the tag name and click the X that appears.

There are a number of ways to share your photos. You can view them on your PC, e-mail them to others, and burn them to CDs and DVDs, just to name a few. And, you know (if you've worked through this book from the beginning) how to do most of this already. Here are a few ideas for sharing photos:

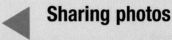
- Use your favourite photo as a Desktop background – In Photo Gallery, right-click any photo and choose Set as desktop background.

- Use a slide show of your photos as a screensaver – Open Personalization, and choose Screen Saver. For Screen saver, select Photos. Click Settings... to choose the folder to use.

Sharing photos (cont.)

E-mail pictures

1 Open Windows Live Photo Gallery.

2 Select pictures to e-mail.

3 Click E-mail.

4 Type the recipient's name(s).

5 Write something in the Subject line.

6 Write something in the body of the e-mail.

7 On the right side of the e-mail, note you can change the resolution of the images.

8 Add other features. Here, I've selected Pushpin.

9 Click Send.

- Print pictures using a photo printer – Click Print in Windows Photo Gallery. Note you can also order prints online.

- Burn a DVD of pictures with Windows DVD Maker – From Photo Gallery, click Make, and click Burn a DVD.

- E-mail photos – In Photo Gallery, select the files to e-mail and click E-mail.

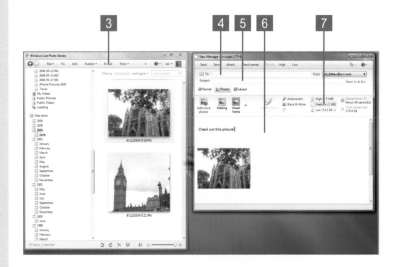

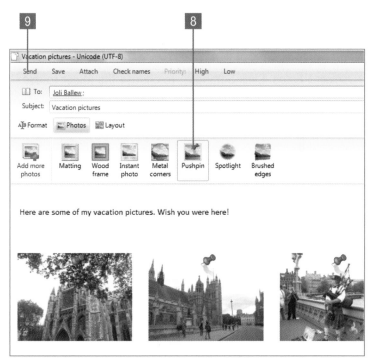

When you send your pictures from Windows Live Gallery, the recipient has the option of viewing those pictures as a slide show. If they choose to do so, they'll see something like this.

Watching DVDs

For your information

If you're downsizing, get rid of that TV/DVD/satellite receiver box combo and use your computer instead!

You can watch a DVD on your computer just as you would on your DVD player and TV. In fact, some people are now getting rid of their home cinema systems in favour of a 'media centre PC' that they connect to their large flat-screen TVs. New PCs built as media computers have television, DVRs, DVD players, music players, speakers, surround sound, and more, installed and ready to use. And the best part is that it's often a more compact option than a combination of television, DVD player, satellite receiver box, DVR, stereo system, speakers, and stacks of DVDs and CDs. That said, it's certainly possible to watch a DVD on your PC; it's one of the most basic entertainment options.

The first time you insert a DVD into the DVD drive, you may be prompted regarding what program to use when playing DVDs; or you may not. The DVD may begin to play automatically in Windows Media Player (this is the most likely option). If you have third-party software installed on the PC that can also play DVDs, the DVD may begin to play in that program.

If prompted, to watch a DVD, simply make a choice. Once the film has started, you'll have access to controls, including fast forward, pause, rewind, stop, resume, volume, and more. Here's a DVD that's playing in Windows Media Player. Windows Media Player was covered earlier in this chapter.

Did you know?

You won't see the controls while the film is playing unless you position your mouse there or access the proper buttons on a remote control.

Although a DVD almost always plays by default in Media Player, you can also play a DVD in Windows Media Center. The controls are very similar to Media Player's controls. To watch a DVD in Media Center, open Media Center, and then navigate to Movies and play dvd.

For your information

Some people prefer Windows Media Center to Windows Media Player. You should experiment with both.

Watch a DVD in Media Center

1 Open Media Center.

2 Navigate to Movies and click play dvd.

3 Insert a DVD into the DVD drive and click OK. Media Player may open and begin playing the DVD, if so, click the X to close Media Player and click play dvd again in Media Center.

4 Hover the mouse over the bottom of the Media Center interface to view the controls.

Burning DVDs with Windows DVD Maker

Windows DVD Maker is an application included with Windows 7 that guides you through the process of burning a DVD that you or anyone else can watch on a TV using a common DVD player. You can also use the program to create menus, scene selection pages, and even slide shows using your favourite songs as a soundtrack. This is an extensive program, and is a much better option when you want to burn a DVD to show others (as opposed to simply backing up data to a DVD). Windows DVD Maker provides a wizard to help you choose what to put on the DVD, to create professional-looking menus and transitions, and to save the data to the DVD so it can be played with a DVD player (not just a DVD drive on a PC). You can find Windows DVD Maker in the Start, All Programs menu.

Getting started

To get started with Windows DVD Maker, you'll add pictures and videos. You can drag and drop these items if you can position the two open windows so that you can access each, or you can click the Add items button on the toolbar. When you click Add items, you then browse to and select the data to add. As you add pictures, they are stored in a folder called Slide Show. You can add pictures and video until you've run out of space on the DVD. There's a nice little icon on the bottom to show you how much space you have left.

Once you've added your data, you can reorder it as desired by dragging and dropping, or by selecting the data and using the up and down buttons on the Toolbar. After you've added your data, you'll create a disk title.

Configuring options

There's a small Options link in the lower right-hand corner of the DVD Maker's window (see right). Click this link to open the Options window (see right). From there, you can configure the program's defaults. Some you may want to consider saving in a specific video format, selecting a DVD burner speed, or choosing the DVD aspect ratio.

Important

Windows DVD Maker requires that your PC meets specific video hardware requirements. If your PC doesn't meet the minimum requirements, you won't be able to use the program.

Did you know?

Images will be played as a slide show when you watch them using your DVD player – in the order they appear in the folder.

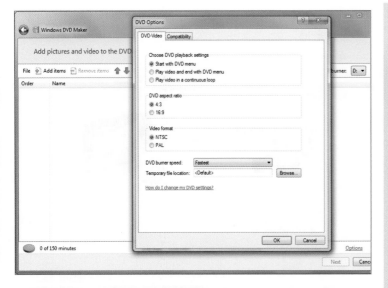

The following options are available:

- Start with DVD menu – Select this option to have your DVD perform like most DVDs you've seen, by displaying a DVD menu when inserted.

- Play video and end with DVD menu – Select this option to have your DVD play the content first and display the menu after the content is complete.

- Play video in a continuous loop – Select this option to have your DVD play in a loop. Users will have to press the Menu button on their DVD remote control or player to access any menus you create.

- DVD aspect ratio – Select a ratio that you think matches what your viewers will use to watch your DVD (or what you will use). A 4:3 aspect is almost square while 16:9 is 'widescreen' or rectangular.

- Video format – Select from NTSC or PAL video format. NTSC format is correct for the United States, but PAL is used in the United Kingdom, Italy, Ireland, Spain and elsewhere.

- Other DVD settings – Select the fastest setting. If you have problems during the burn process, choose a slower speed.

Burning DVDs with Windows DVD Maker (cont.)

Create a professional DVD with Windows DVD Maker (part I)

Here, we'll make a DVD from a video on the PC, but note that you can also select pictures to create a slide show too. There will be notes regarding this throughout.

1. Click Start.

2. Click All programs.

3. Click Windows DVD Maker.

4. Click Choose Photos and Videos (if prompted by the welcome page).

5. Click Add items.

6. Browse to the data you want to add. You might choose something from the Videos or Sample Videos folder as shown here.

7. Select the video to add, click Add.

For your information

Type a new name for the disk at the bottom of the DVD Maker interface. By default, it's today's date.

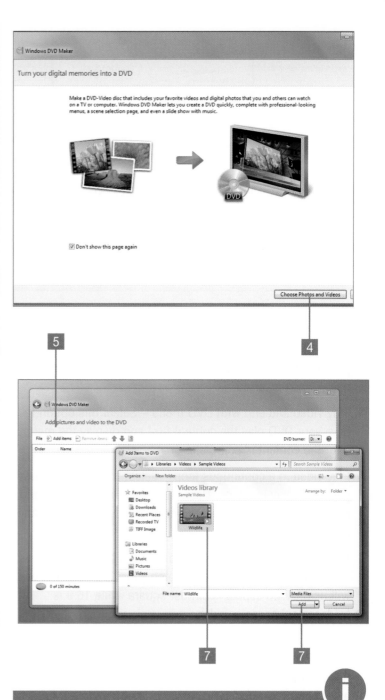

For your information

If you want to make changes to the options, click Options. In the DVD Options window, make changes as desired and click OK.

For your information

Click Organize in the Add items to DVD window to access options like Select all.

For your information

You can choose individual images, but you can't choose entire folders. If you choose images, the DVD will offer a slideshow of pictures.

8 Click Add items again.

9 Choose some pictures and click Add. Leave this open to continue to part II – the next task

Menus, text, foreground and background video, Scenes button, and more

Once you've added your data and clicked Next, you'll have additional options for personalising your DVD. You can skip all of it if you like, or you can go crazy, spending hours tweaking menus and such. You can also preview the DVD (always a good idea), add music and change options for the slide show.

At the very least, you should click Preview to see how the film will look prior to burning it to a DVD.

Burning DVDs with Windows DVD Maker (cont.)

If you want to spend more time here, click the Menu text button. You can change the font and its attributes, the title and the text used for the Play, Scenes and Notes. You can also write your own personalised note! You can make changes using the Customize menu toolbar button. You can add foreground and background video, and even audio, or change the Scenes button style. You should also browse through the Menu styles list. You can choose from several, including Special occasion, and you can view a preview.

Finally, click the Slide show button to change any slide show settings. This includes adding music and animation, as well as choosing how one picture transitions into another.

Once you're ready, and make sure you've previewed your movie, click the Burn button. Insert a blank disk into the drive, and wait while the DVD Maker creates the disk.

Create a professional DVD with Windows DVD Maker (part II)

Continuing from Step 9 in the previous task, click Next. You can then click Preview, Burn or continue here.

10 Click File, and click Save as. (If something happens, you can reopen this file later.)

11 Type a file name.

12 Note that, by default, the file will save in the Videos folder of your personal folder. Click Save.

13 Make a selection from the Menu Styles list. I've chosen Special Occasion. Note that, at any point, you can click Burn to complete the DVD. You do not have to personalise the DVD.

14 If desired, click Menu text.

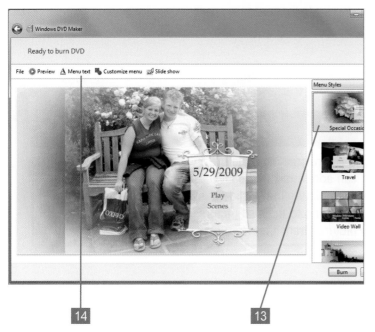

For your information

Click Preview any time to review your project in progress.

Burning DVDs with Windows DVD Maker (cont.)

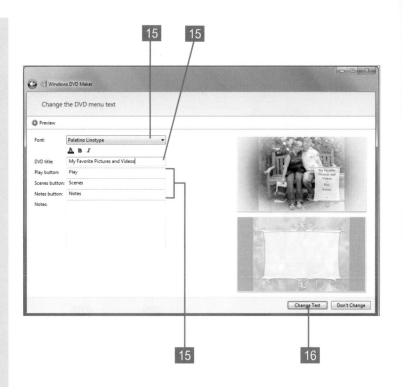

15 Select a font from the drop-down list. Change the DVD title, and choose a different word to represent Play, Scenes or Notes. (For instance, you might change Notes to Disclaimer or Read This First!)

16 Click Change Text.

17 Click Customize menu.

18 Click Browse to select a foreground video, background video or menu audio if desired. Locate the file and click Open to add it.

19 Select a new Scenes button style.

20 Click Change Style.

21 Click Burn and follow the prompts to insert a DVD and finalise the burn process.

For your information

If you're creating a picture DVD, click Slide show. You can add music to the DVD, assign how many seconds each picture in the slide show should appear before changing to the next picture, and choose how the pictures transition from one to the other.

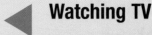

Windows Media Center is a one-stop media application that lets you access and manage pictures, videos, films, music, online media, television, DVDs and CDs, and radio. As you already know though, you can do much of this elsewhere. You can manage pictures in Windows Live Photo Gallery; manage music, online media, radio stations and portable devices in Media Player; and you can create DVDs using Windows DVD Maker. So where does Media Center shine then, and how should you use it?

Media Center, although it can be used to listen to music, really stands out for viewing, recording, watching and managing television, obtaining and viewing online media, and watching DVDs you own or rent. It's a 'media centre' if you will, a place to enjoy the media you already have access to and have already 'managed'. Media Center has an online guide to help you find out what's available to watch and when too, and you can record television programs, pause live TV, and then fast forward or rewind through what you've paused.

You should start with Media Center by watching and recording TV, and then move on to watching DVDs and online media. As time passes and you get more comfortable with Media Center, you may find you prefer it over Media Player and Windows Live Photo Gallery. How far to take it is up to you!

Once Media Center is set up and you know how to navigate through it, it's simple to watch TV. Just browse to TV, and click Live TV. If everything is set up and installed as it should be, you'll get a live TV signal. And once you have a live TV signal, it's almost as easy to get started recording TV.

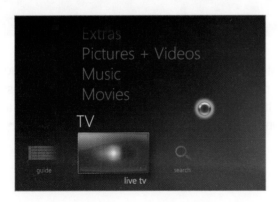

Watching TV (cont.)

Watching live TV

When you're watching live TV, you'll see the broadcast, of course, but other items will appear and disappear, seemingly at will. As you can see here, the channel number as well as the show's name (among other things) appears as do familiar-looking controls.

The show's broadcast information appears when you change to the channel, and you can also bring it up by right-clicking in that area of the screen. When you right-click you'll not only get the show information but other options as well. Note here that program info is selected, but there's also details, zoom, and captions (not shown).

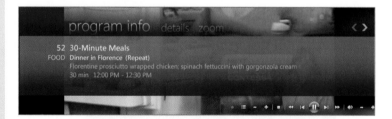

There are also TV controls. These controls appear when you move your mouse to the bottom of the screen, if you press specific buttons on a remote control or keyboard, and in a few other instances. With these controls you can:

- Record the show you're watching by pressing the red Record button.

- Change the channel using the Channel up and Channel down buttons.

- Stop watching TV using the Stop button.

- Rewind quickly or more slowly using the two Rewind buttons.

- Pause (and then Play) live TV using the Pause/Play button.

- Fast forward slowly or more quickly using the two Fast forward buttons.

- Mute the TV by clicking the Mute button.

- Decrease or increase the volume using the Volume down and Volume up buttons.

For your information

You can pause live TV. Pausing is great for skipping through commercials. Just pause the TV for a while at any point and when commercials come on, simply fast forward through them.

Watch live TV in Media Center

1. Open Media Center.

2. Click TV.

3. Click live tv.

4. Experiment with the Channel up and Channel down buttons.

5. Click Pause. Wait a few minutes.

6. Click Play.

7. Mute and unmute the sounds.

8. Change the volume using the Volume up and Volume down buttons.

9. Fast forward and rewind using the Fast forward and Rewind buttons.

Recording TV

There are a lot of ways to access the commands to Record and Record Series. As you learned in the previous section, you can record a live TV show by clicking the red Record button at the bottom of the screen. You won't always want to record what you're watching though; you are more likely to want to record something that is coming on later in the week. That's what the Guide is for. And while there are multiple ways to access the Guide, the most straightforward is from the TV menu you're already familiar with. (You can also open the Guide using a remote control or media keyboard if you have one.)

Right-click any show listed in the Guide to see the following options:

- Program Details (left) – displays information about the show, including the date and time it will be aired, the channel it's on, and a brief synopsis. You can also record and record a series from this screen.

- Record – Immediately starts recording the current television show or the singular instance of it in the Guide.

For your information

Click the Back button to return to a previous screen. The Back button will appear when you position the mouse in the top left corner of the screen.

- Record Series – Immediately starts recording the current television show and schedules the television series to be recorded.

- Search – Opens the search options where you can search for a show based on its title, keyword, categories, actor or director.

- View Categories – Opens the categories option on the Guide where you can filter Guide results by Most Viewed, Movies, Sports, Kids, and more.

- Edit Channel – Lets you change the channel number of the selected channel. You can also edit listings, preview shows, and more.

- Settings (overleaf) – Opens Media Center Settings. Options include General, TV, Pictures, Music, DVD, Start Menu and Extras, Extender, and Media Libraries.

Recording TV (cont.)

Record a TV show or series in Media Center

1 Click TV and scroll right to Guide.

2 Use your mouse, arrows on the keyboard or another method to locate the show to record.

3 Right-click the program.

4 Select Record or Record Series.

You move through the Guide using the arrow keys on your keyboard, a scroll wheel on a mouse or a remote control. You can click with the mouse on these arrows to move through the Guide as well. The arrow will appear when you hover the mouse over that particular area of the screen.

Important

!

Remember, you can always click the Back arrow (it will appear when you hover the mouse over the top left-hand corner) to return to the previous screen.

Watching a recorded TV show

To watch a TV show you've recorded, simply browse to TV, recorded tv and click the recorded show you want to watch! As you can see here, you can also add a recording, view scheduled recordings and browse by title. It's just as easy as watching live TV.

There's a new kid on the block and its name is online media. Seriously, you must check it out. Online media services offer everything your local DVD rental shop does, without the long queues, teenagers and 'out-of-stock' notices. It's better than renting through the post too, since you don't have to wait for anything to arrive. Additionally, most offer a 14-day free trial, and monthly fees are very reasonable. You can also subscribe to services like Netflix, which allows you to download and watch media instantly. You'll have to have a subscription, but with these services, you're in charge of what you want to watch and when.

You can begin to explore some of these media options under Extras. One must-see feature is internet tv. Also explore the extras library, news and extras gallery. When you've finished with that, scroll down to music and then sports, to round out your Media Center experience.

Networking

Introduction

Windows 7 offers plenty of ways to network (connect) multiple computers. If you have more than one computer in your home, you should consider connecting them. With all of your computers networked, you can share data, printers and an Internet connection.

Creating a network from scratch can seem daunting though, especially if you're new to computing. However, if you already have a broadband Internet connection through a cable or DSL modem on a single PC, it isn't too hard to add a router and share that connection. And, if you have a dial-up or satellite connection to the Internet and no additional hardware, it's equally easy to purchase a crossover cable and physically connect the two computers to create a network. If it's a wireless network you're after, that takes a bit more know-how; however, Windows 7's networking options may be able to walk you through it. (If not, you can always ask a teenager for help!)

Windows 7 offers the following to help you get started:

- Network and Sharing Center – A collection of features where you can easily access network connections, sharing options, networked computers and devices, and diagnose and repair features.

- HomeGroups – A simple way to share data on networked PCs that run Windows 7.

- Network – A place to easily access computers on your network and the Network and Sharing Center. You can also add printers and wireless devices here.

What you'll do

Add Windows 7 to an existing network or set up a new one

Set up an Ethernet network

Set up a wireless network

Begin the set-up

Create a homegroup

Join a homegroup

Share a personal folder

- Network map – A map that details each of your network connections graphically, and allows you to distinguish easily among wired, wireless and Internet connections.

- Network Setup Wizard – A wizard to create a new network, be it Ethernet, direct or wireless.

When you connect a Windows 7 PC to a wired network or get within range of a wireless one (and you have wireless hardware installed in your computer), Windows 7 will find the network and then ask you what kind of network it is. (Windows 7 is always looking for networks.) It's a public network if you're in a coffee shop, library or café, and it's a private network if it's a network you manage, like one already in your home. Connecting to an existing network allows you to access shared features of the network. In a coffee shop that's probably only a connection to the Internet; if it's a home network, it's your personal, shared data (and probably a connection to the Internet too).

When a network is accessible for the first time, either because you've connected to it using an 'Ethernet' cable or through a wireless network card inside your PC, you will be prompted to connect.

There are three network options and, when prompted, you need to select one. Here's how to know which one to choose:

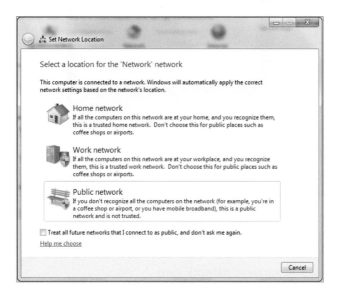

- Home network – Choose this if the network is your home network or a network you trust (like a network at your children's house). This connection type lets your computer *discover* other PCs, printers and devices on the network and they can 'see' you.

 12

Jargon buster

Network – two or more computers that are connected physically or wirelessly for the purpose of sharing resources like music, videos, an Internet connection, documents, pictures, and more.

Ethernet – a special cable that you use to connect a PC to a router, cable modem, DSL modem, hub, switch, or other specialised networking device.

Connecting to a network (cont.)

Did you know?

To see network connectivity information, hover the mouse over the network icon on the Taskbar. Click the network icon to see what's shown here.

- Work network – Choose this if you are connecting to a network at work. The settings for Work and Home are the same, only the titles differ so you can tell them apart easily.

- Public network – Choose this if the network you want to connect to is open to anyone within range of it, like networks in cafés, airports and libraries. Windows 7 works out that if you choose Public, you only want to connect to the Internet and nothing else. It closes down *discoverability*, so that even your shared data is safe.

After successfully connecting to a network, one of three network icons will appear in the Notification area of the Taskbar:

- Connected with network and Internet access – You are connected to the local network and the Internet. You can access shared data on the local network. This is the one you want to see at home.

- Connected with local (network) access only – You are connected to the local network and can access shared local resources and data, but you do not have Internet access.

- Disconnected – You are not connected to the Internet or a local network. This is generally due to a break somewhere in the process, like a router that's been turned off or a disabled wireless network card.

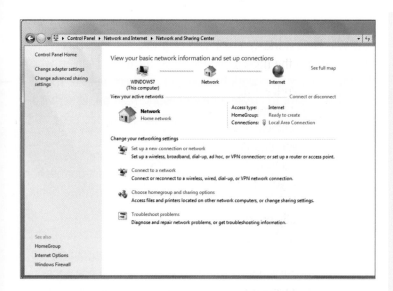

If you're prompted about setting up a homegroup, refer to the Homegroups section of this chapter for more information.

Add Windows 7 to an existing network or set up a new one

12

1 Physically connect to a wired network using an Ethernet cable or, if you have wireless hardware installed in your PC, get within range of a wireless network.

2 Select Home, Work, or Public Location when prompted. (If necessary input credentials.)

3 You will see that the network was set up in the Notification area and in the Network and Sharing Center. (You'll learn more about this later.)

Types of networks

If you already have a network set up, and you've joined your new Windows 7 PC to it, you can skip this section. This section and the section following it are for those readers who do not yet have a network but would like to create one. That said, if you want to create a new network, read on. Otherwise, skip to the section The Network and Sharing Center, page 308.

While there are many ways to connect two or more PCs, I'll suggest you choose from one of these three: direct connection, Ethernet or wireless. Let's look at each of these in more detail.

Direct connection

If you have only two computers, do not want to purchase expensive equipment and you trust everyone who has access to those two computers, you may want to consider a direct connection network. This is an older technology though, and thus the connection between the two computers will be much slower than newer alternatives. However, if you don't want to purchase expensive equipment, this is the way to go. Often you only need to purchase one thing: an Ethernet crossover cable.

For this method to work, both computers must be able to connect to an Ethernet cable. That means each computer must either have a network interface card (NIC) or a USB port for attaching a USB-to-Ethernet converter.

Note: An Ethernet port looks about the same as the port you use to connect your telephone to a wall socket or a phone cord to a modem in the PC; the Ethernet port is just a big larger.

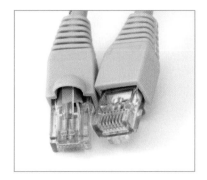

I will venture to say that all computers with Windows 7 pre-installed will have the required NIC, but it's possible older computers do not. If you want to use this method but don't have an Ethernet port in one of the PCs, purchase and install an external USB-to-Ethernet converter. (If you don't have a USB port, there are additional options like serial-to-Ethernet adapters.) Once connected, you can share an Internet connection and data, just as you can with any network.

Note: Another option for connecting two PCs directly is to use a USB-to-USB direct link cable. Microsoft offers the Easy Transfer cable that can be used for this purpose. If both PCs have a USB port, consider this option.

Ethernet

If you have more than two computers to network, consider an Ethernet network. Ethernet networks connect computers through a hardware device like a router. A router is a small piece of external hardware that offers multiple Ethernet ports for plugging in multiple computers and 'routes' the data flowing through the network from PC to PC. Routers come in 4-port, 6-port and similar varieties. Ethernet networks are fast too, and are a good option when sharing a broadband Internet connection. The Network Map, available in the Network and Sharing Center, shows your hardware.

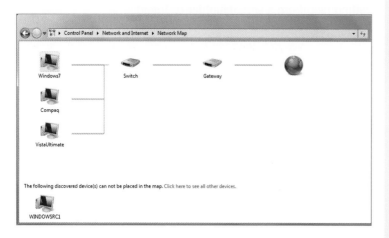

Types of networks (cont.)

The downside here is that you have to purchase a router and cables, and you have to set it up (or pay someone to do it). Often this entails adding a cable modem to the mix too, so you have to know how to position the equipment. While routers come with instructions, it can be a time-consuming and frustrating task, so if you're new to routers, cable modems and networking, have the network professionally installed or call on your children or friends to help. If you want to set it up yourself though, no worries. I'll include some generic instructions shortly.

Wireless

Wireless networks are the third option. Wireless networks use radio waves, just like mobile phones and walkie-talkies, and allow you to connect to your networked PCs without cables. If you have a laptop with a built in wireless card, this is the way to go. If you have older computers that do not have wireless capabilities, you can still make it work. Just get a wireless router that offers a few Ethernet ports. Additionally, you could purchase a USB adapter or PCI card for any computer not wireless-ready. While this network is great once it's set up, like any new network, getting it up and running can be time-consuming and frustrating. Instructions that come with the hardware in my experience at least, are clear, but if you've never done this type of thing before, consider having it professionally installed or getting help from a son, daughter or friend.

Here is Device Manager, which you can search for from the Search dialogue box. Notice under Network adapters that only one adapter is installed. In this case, it's for Ethernet. In order to connect to a wireless network from this computer, you'd have to install a wireless adapter.

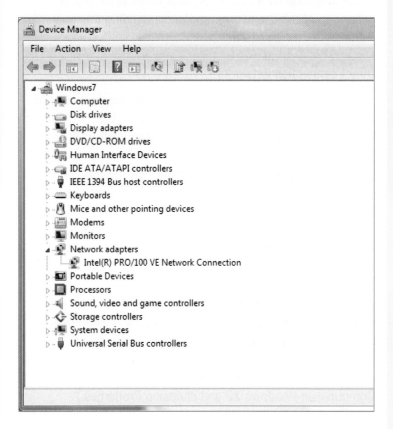

12

If you see two items listed under Network adapters in Device Manager, it's highly probable one is a wireless adapter.

Physically installing new network hardware

Because of the different types of routers, networking hardware and configurations, there's no way I can walk you through physically installing every type of network hardware here. The hardware you purchase will come with specific instructions anyway, and set-up is not always the same from manufacturer to manufacturer. However, I can offer information that is generic to specific networks, and understanding this may make installing hardware easier.

Direct connection networks

When creating a direct connection network, you first need to connect the two PCs using the desired cable (Easy Transfer or Ethernet crossover). You may have to also install USB-to-Ethernet converters if your PCs don't have Ethernet ports, but almost all computers have these. Once you make the connection, Windows 7 will attempt to configure it, and you'll be prompted when a network is available. Once a network is available, you can tweak it using the Network and Sharing Center. There will be more on that later.

Note: Computers in the same 'workgroup' can communicate more easily than those that are not. By default, Windows 7 names a workgroup WORKGROUP. If you can't see other computers on your network, consider changing their workgroup names to WORKGROUP. (You can do this by right-clicking Computer on Windows 7 and Windows Vista, or My Computer on Windows XP and choosing Properties.)

Ethernet networks

Direct connection networks generally only require the installation of a single cable, but Ethernet networks require much more setting up. Although there's no way to outline how to install the hardware for any Ethernet hardware, the steps usually need to be performed in the order detailed in the task, right.

Wireless networks

During the process of configuring your wireless router, you'll also set up your wireless network. You'll want to follow the directions that come with your wireless hardware, which often begin with the direction to install the wireless router's software. As with Ethernet networks, you'll need to make sure you have a working, wired (not wireless) connection to the Internet before starting. Once software is installed, you'll be prompted to physically install the hardware.

The hardware you need to install a wireless network includes:

- A wireless router (also called an access point).

- A wireless network adapter for each computer on your network.

- An installation CD.

- External cable, DSL or satellite modem.

Physically installing new network hardware (cont.)

Set up an Ethernet network

1 Set up any satellite, cable or broadband modems and connect one of the PCs to the Internet. This may already be done.

2 Set up the router as detailed in the instructions that come with it. For the most part you'll need to:

   a. Install the router software.

   b. Connect the router to the external cable or satellite modem through the router's WAN port.

   c. Connect the PC to an available Ethernet port on the router.

   d Run the set-up wizard provided by the router manufacturer and work through the wizard and/or follow the written directions.

   e. During set-up, if prompted regarding how your ISP obtains an IP address, choose Obtain an IP address automatically. If you have problems with this step, call your ISP.

12

Physically installing new network hardware (cont.)

3 Once the router is configured, turn off the PC, cable or satellite modem, and router.

4 Turn on the modem and wait for all self-tests to complete.

5 Turn on the router and wait for all self-tests to complete.

6 Turn on each PC.

During set-up you'll be prompted to create a Wireless Network Name (SSID), passphrase or password, and security settings. Don't worry, there's almost always a wizard to guide you through this. However, just to be on the safe side, here are few terms you should be familiar with:

- SSID – This is the name you create and use for the wireless network during set-up.

- Channel – This denotes the operating frequency your wireless network will use. Don't worry, this will probably have been configured automatically.

- Mode – This is where you'll tell set-up what type of wireless hardware you are using (G, B, A, etc., but you can simply choose Auto to let the software configure all of that for you.

- Encryption – This is the security you'll apply to your network. You can choose:

  - none – no data encryption;

  - WEP – Wired Equivalent Privacy, 64-bit or 128-bit options: 64-bit WEP uses 10 hexadecimal digits (0–9 and A–F) for a password; 128-bit uses 26 hexadecimal digits;

  - Security Encryption (WPA-PSK, WPA2-PSK, WPA-PSK+WPA2-PSK) – Wi-Fi Protected Access with Pre-Shared Key – the Passphrase is 8 to 63 characters in length.

This isn't nearly as complicated as it sounds though – for the most part all of this will happen automatically. During set-up you'll also be prompted to install the hardware. Again, instructions will be included but generically you'll perform the steps shown in the task.

Once the network is set up, all you have to do is wait for Windows 7 to discover the network, and prompt you to join. If necessary, reread the task Add Windows 7 to an existing network or set up a new one, page 297, to review how this works.

Set up a wireless network

1. Place the router near the centre of the area where all your PCs will operate. Make sure it's elevated so all PCs have access to its wireless signal. Keep the router away from microwaves and similar devices.

2. Verify a cable modem is installed and connected to the Internet.

3. Connect an Ethernet cable from the Ethernet out socket on the modem to the WAN port on the wireless router.

4. Connect an Ethernet cable from the Windows 7 PC to the wireless router.

5. Complete any additional instructions.

12

Setting up a connection or network

Once your hardware is installed, you may need to tell Windows 7 you want to set up the network. (In some cases, the computers seem to recognise each other without assistance from you, though.) You'll use the Network and Sharing Center to do this.

For your information

You may already be connected to a network. This may have happened when you set up your Internet connection. There's no need to continue if you're already part of the network you want to join.

Begin the set-up

To access the Network and Sharing Center and begin set up:

1. Click Start, and in the Search dialogue box, type Network and Sharing.
2. Click Network and Sharing Center.
3. Click Set up a new connection or network.

From the Network and Sharing Center options, choose Set up a connection or network. Options include:

- Connect to the Internet – Choose this to set up a wireless, wired or dial-up connection to the Internet.

- Set up a new network – Choose this to set up a wireless router or access point. The wizard should detect your network hardware and settings, and guide you through any remaining set-up tasks.

- Connect to a workplace – Choose this option if you need to create a VPN (virtual private network). Chances are you'll never need to do this. If you ever do need to create a VPN, it's more likely a tech support person will set it up for you, or at least give you directions. This is more of a corporate networking solution.

- Set up a dial-up connection – Choose this if you want to connect using a dial-up Internet connection via a telephone line and computer modem. Most dial-up providers offer their own software though, and if that's the case, use it instead of this.

- Manually connect to a wireless network – Choose this to connect to a wireless network that was not automatically found by Windows 7. In these cases, you'll generally have to input security information, like a security key (passcode).

- Set up a wireless ad hoc (computer-to-computer) network –
  Choose this to set up a temporary peer-to-peer network
  between two PCs within close range, both of which have
  wireless adapters. This allows for temporary transfer of data.

- Connect to a Bluetooth personal area network – Choose
  this if you need to create a temporary network between a
  Bluetooth-capable PC and a Bluetooth-capable device. This
  may be a smart phone, Blackberry or something similar.

You may only see the four options shown in this figure, or you
may see more depending on the hardware or edition you're
using.

Once you select an option, simply follow the prompts to set up
your network. (What you'll see depends on what option you
select, and the wizard will walk you through the required steps.)

The Network and Sharing Center

Once your network is configured, or at least physically connected, you can tweak the network using the Network and Sharing Center. The Network and Sharing Center contains links and access to everything you'll need to configure and manage your network. You access the Network and Sharing Center by clicking the Network icon in the Notification area on the Taskbar or from the Network window, among other places. The Network and Sharing Center offers lots of features. These features are briefly outlined here.

The main Network and Sharing Center window contains options for viewing network connections and changing default settings. These include:

- Network map – A network map is a graphical representation of the network that shows the relationship between your computer, the local network and the Internet. Red Xs indicate a problem with the network connection. If you don't see any red Xs, the network is functioning properly.

- Active networks – This list shows all of the connected networks. You can have more than one. For instance, you might have one connection to the Internet and another to a local network.

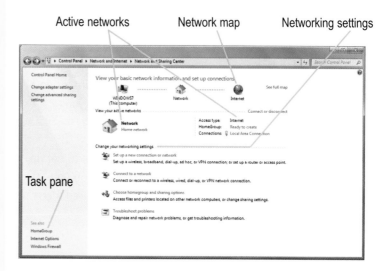

Active networks Network map Networking settings

Task pane

- Networking settings – This list offers options for connecting to a network or troubleshooting one. There's Set up a new connection or network, Connect to a network, Choose homegroup and sharing options (more on this later) and Troubleshoot problems.

On the left of the Network and Sharing Center is the Task pane. You can access Control Panel, change adapter settings or change advanced sharing settings. You'll probably access the advanced settings more than the other two.

Select Change advanced sharing settings to access options for your network (or networks):

- Network discovery – This section lets you configure options related to network discovery. These settings are configured automatically based on the network type you choose when you connected (Home, Work, Public Location). However, you can override those settings here, and configure additional settings.

- File and printer sharing – This section offers settings for the shared data you've set up yourself and printers you've installed and shared. File and printer sharing is on in private networks and off in public ones.

Did you know?

Network discovery is on in private networks and off in public ones.

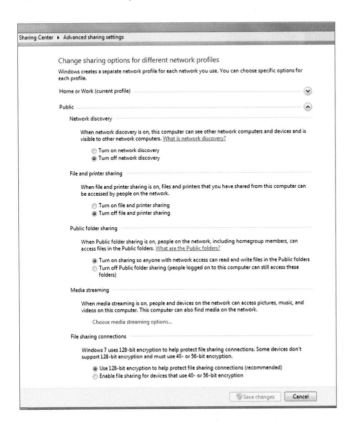

Sharing Center ▸ Advanced sharing settings

Change sharing options for different network profiles

Windows creates a separate network profile for each network you use. You can choose specific options for each profile.

Home or Work (current profile)

Public

Network discovery

When network discovery is on, this computer can see other network computers and devices and is visible to other network computers. What is network discovery?

○ Turn on network discovery
◉ Turn off network discovery

File and printer sharing

When file and printer sharing is on, files and printers that you have shared from this computer can be accessed by people on the network.

○ Turn on file and printer sharing
◉ Turn off file and printer sharing

Public folder sharing

When Public folder sharing is on, people on the network, including homegroup members, can access files in the Public folders. What are the Public folders?

◉ Turn on sharing so anyone with network access can read and write files in the Public folders
○ Turn off Public folder sharing (people logged on to this computer can still access these folders)

Media streaming

When media streaming is on, people and devices on the network can access pictures, music, and videos on this computer. This computer can also find media on the network.

Choose media streaming options...

File sharing connections

Windows 7 uses 128-bit encryption to help protect file sharing connections. Some devices don't support 128-bit encryption and must use 40- or 56-bit encryption.

◉ Use 128-bit encryption to help protect file sharing connections (recommended)
○ Enable file sharing for devices that use 40- or 56-bit encryption

Save changes   Cancel

The Network and Sharing Center (cont.)

Important

!

Learn how to create and join a homegroup next.

- Public folder sharing – This section offers a way to turn public folder sharing on or off. If you turn public folder sharing on, any data you put in shared folders will be available to network users.

- Media streaming – This section allows you to enable media sharing so others on the network can access shared media.

- File sharing connections – This section lets you configure encryption methods for shared data. You won't need to do anything here.

- Password protected sharing – This section allows you to enable sharing but requires a password. Users who have access to the network are required to input a user name password before accessing shared resources.

- HomeGroup connections – Homegroup computers are computers you assign to a homegroup. Typically, Windows manages this. However, you can manually manage homegroup settings by selecting Use user accounts and passwords to connect to other computers. I don't suggest changing this.

?

Did you know?

A homegroup lets you easily share music, pictures and documents among home computers. You can create a homegroup as soon as you set up your network if you choose Home network in the Set Network Location window.

A homegroup is a new feature in Windows 7 that allows you to simplify the task of sharing media, documents, printers and other data on your home network with other PCs that are also running Windows 7. You may have created a homegroup during the network set-up process, outlined in the first section of this chapter. However, if you did not create a homegroup then or if you're on another Windows 7 PC and want to join the homegroup you created, you can do so from the Network and Sharing Center.

Homegroups

Create a homegroup

1 Click the Network icon in the Taskbar's Notification area.

2 Click Open Network and Sharing Center.

3 Under View your active networks, locate HomeGroup and click Ready to create. If you see Joined, you've already created a homegroup. If you see Available to join, skip to the next task.

12

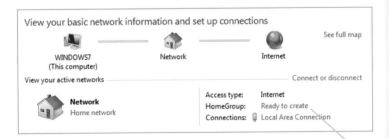

Homegroups
(cont.)

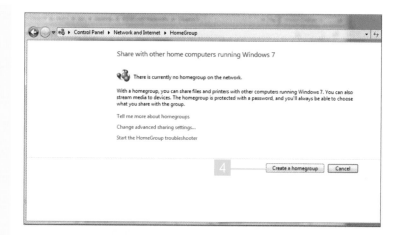

4   Click Create a homegroup.

5   Select the items to share. By default, Pictures, Music, Videos and Printers are selected and Documents are not. Click Create now.

6   Write down the password and click Finish.

7   The Change homegroup settings windows will remain open. You can make changes as desired, or simply click Cancel.

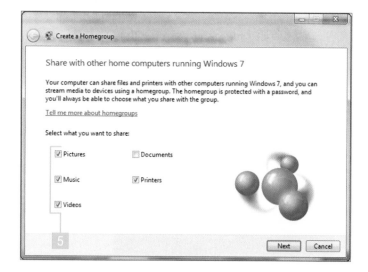

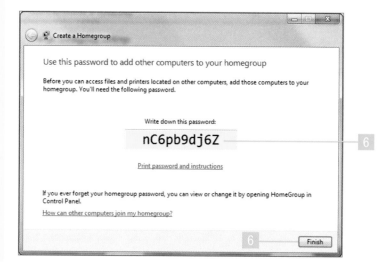

Did you know?

You can view the homegroup password from Control Panel, Network and Internet, HomeGroup if you forget it. You can also change the password here.

For your information

You'll only need to join a homegroup if you have created one on a Windows 7 PC and you are adding a second Windows 7 PC to the network.

Join a homegroup

1 On the second Windows 7 PC, open the Network and Sharing Center.

2 Under View your active networks, click Available to join.

3 Click Join now.

4 Type the homegroup password.

5 Choose the data you'd like to share.

6 Click Join now, and Finish.

12

Sharing data

The main reasons people create a network is to share data, printers, media and an Internet connection. In this section, we'll talk about sharing data. There are three ways to share data: you can share data automatically among Windows 7 PCs using a homegroup, put the data you want to share in the built-in Public folders or you can share data using personal folders you create. You can use a combination of these as well. How do you know which to use and when? Here are some things to take into consideration.

Homegroups

Homegroups are the easiest way to share music, pictures and documents in your home network. However, homegroups require that all the PCs run Windows 7, and that's not usually the case. With homegroups you can share your USB-connected printers and other hardware more easily too. If the PCs on your home network all run Windows 7 (or higher), create a homegroup on one of them, and join the homegroup from the others. Each user can decide when joining the homegroup what they want to share with others on the network.

Public folder sharing

Public folders are already built into the Windows 7 folder structure. The Public folder contains several subfolders, including Public Documents, Public Downloads, Public Music, Public Pictures, Recorded TV and Public Videos. You can create your own folders here too. To share data using the folders, simply save or place the data there. Then, anyone who has access to the computer or network can access what's in the folders easily.

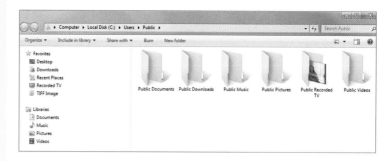

Use the Public folder for sharing if:

- You want every person with a user account on the computer to be able to access what's in the folder.

- You want to share files and folders from a single location on your PC – if you choose to use your personal folders, shared data will not all be stored in a central location.

- You want to be able to access, view and modify everything you have shared quickly.

- You want everything you are sharing kept separate from the data you do not want to share.

- You do not need to configure different sharing rules for different people who have access – you are OK with everyone having access to the data, and everyone being able to do what they wish with it.

- You prefer to use the default shared settings and do not want manually to share data.

You can locate the Public folders by typing Public in the Search window. You can also right-click the Public folders icon, and choose Send To, and then Desktop to create a shortcut to the folder on your PC's Desktop.

Personal folder sharing

Your personal folders and any folders you create yourself can be shared. In contrast to using Public folders for sharing, with personal folder sharing you have much more control over the shared data.

Use any folder for sharing if:

- You want to share data directly from your personal folders, like Documents, Pictures or Music, and do not want to have to resave or move data you want to share to your Public folder.

Sharing data (cont.)

- You want to allow some users the ability to change the data in the shared folders while at the same time only allowing others to view it, plus you want to completely block others from accessing the data at all. (You can't do this with Public folder sharing.)

- You share large files that would be burdensome to copy and manage in a separate shared folder.

Share a personal folder

1. Locate a folder to share. In this example, I'll share the My Documents folder.

2. Right-click the folder.

3. Click Share with.

4. Select Nobody, Homegroup (Read), Homegroup (Read/Write) or Specific people... If you choose to share with a homegroup, you're done.

Permissions for shared folders

When you share a folder, you can configure who can access the folder by right-clicking it. Click Share with to see your options. After selecting an option, you can configure other sharing details, if applicable.

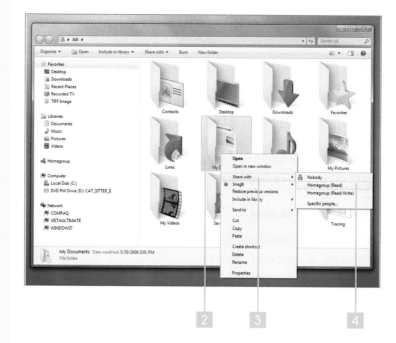

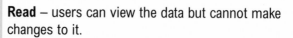

Jargon buster

Read – users can view the data but cannot make changes to it.

Read/Write – users can view and change the shared data.

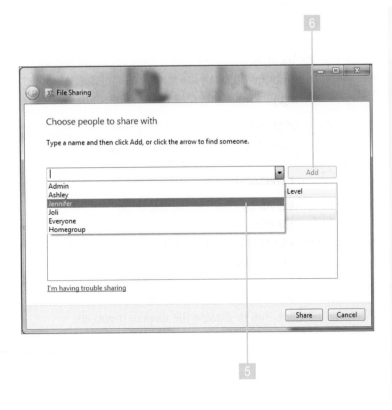

Sharing data (cont.)

12

5 If you choose to share a folder with specific people then click the down arrow in the File Sharing dialogue box and select a name.

6 Click Add.

7 Click the down arrow by the new user's name to select a permission level.

8 Click Share.

Managing network connections

Connections is an option in the Network and Sharing Center. There, you can see the connections you use on your PC. On a home PC, this is most probably only a local area connection, as shown here. Click it to open the connection status window. Here the connections name is Local Area Connection.

In the status window you can do the following:

- Properties – Click this to change the settings of the connection. You probably won't need to be here very often, if at all.

- Disable – Click this to disable the device. If you are connected to a network through this device, you'll be disconnected.

- Diagnose – Use this to start the Windows Network Diagnostics wizard.

Jargon buster

Router – a piece of equipment used to send data from computer to computer on a network. A router 'routes' the data to the correct PC and also rejects data that is harmful or from unknown sources.

Ethernet cable – a cable that is used to connect PCs to routers and cable modems, among other things.

Network Discovery – a state where computers can find other computers on the network. Network Discover must be on to locate and communicate with network devices.

Network – a group of computers, printers and other devices that communicate wirelessly or through wired connections.

Permissions – rules associated with a shared resource, like a folder, file or printer.

Jargon buster

Action Center – A new feature in Windows 7 that allows you to view problems, fix problems and run automated troubleshooters.

Activation – The process you must complete to verify you have a valid copy of Windows 7, including a proper Product ID. You usually activate Windows 7 online, the first time you turn on the PC. This is mandatory.

Address bar – In Internet Explorer or any web browser, this is where you type in Internet addresses, also known as URLs (uniform resource locators). Generally, an Internet address takes the form of *http://www.companyname.com*.

Adware – Internet advertisements (which are also applications) that often include additional code that can be used to track a user's personal information and pass it on to third parties, without the user's authorisation or knowledge.

Aero – Windows Aero builds on the basic Windows 7 interface and offers a high-performing desktop experience that includes (among other things) the translucent effect of Aero Glass.

Aero Glass – Added visual reflections and soft animations that are applied when Aero is selected as the display setting.

Applications – Software installed on your PC other than the operating system. Some applications come pre-installed, like Windows Calendar, Windows DVD Maker and Internet Explorer. Third-party applications are software you purchase separately and install yourself, like Microsoft Office or Photoshop.

Attachment – An attachment is something you add to an e-mail, such as a photograph, a short video, a sound recording, document or other data. There are many ways to attach something to an e-mail.

Backup and Restore Center – This feature lets you perform back-ups and, in the case of a computer failure, restore them (put them back). However, there are other back-up options too, including copying files to a CD or DVD, copying pictures and media to an external hard drive, USB drive or memory card, or storing them on an Internet server.

Bandwidth – Generally this is used to represent how much data you send and receive on a paid connection, like a smart phone or Internet connection.

Bcc – If you want to send an e-mail to someone and you don't want other recipients to know you included them in the e-mail, add them to the Bcc line. Bcc stands for blind carbon copy and is a secret copy.

Boot up – When a computer is switched on, it goes through a sequence of tasks before you see the Desktop. This process is called the booting-up process. Computers can be rated by many factors, and one of those factors is how long the booting-up process takes.

Browse – Browsing for a file, folder or program is the process of drilling down into the operating system's folder structure to locate the desired item.

Burn – A term used to describe the process of copying music from a computer to a CD or DVD. Generally music is burned to a CD, since CDs can be played in cars and generic CD players, and videos are burned to DVDs since they require much more space and can be played on DVD players.

Cc – If you want to send an e-mail to someone and you don't need them to respond, you can put them in the Cc line. Cc stands for carbon copy. (Bcc is a blind carbon copy; other recipients cannot see the Bcc field address.)

Contacts folder – This folder contains your contacts' information, which includes e-mail addresses, pictures, phone numbers, home and businesses addresses, and more.

Control Panel – A place where you can change computer settings related to system and maintenance, user accounts, security, appearance, networks and the Internet, the time, language and region, hardware and sounds, visual displays and accessibility options, programs and additional options.

Cookies – These are small text files that include data that identifies your preferences when you visit particular websites. Cookies are what allow you to visit, say, *www.amazon.com* and be greeted with 'Hello <your name>, We have recommendations for you!' Cookies help a site offer you a personalised web experience.

Copy command – Copies the data to the Clipboard (a virtual, temporary holding area). The data will be not deleted from its original location even when you 'paste' it somewhere else. Pasting copy data will copy the data, not move it.

Cut – Use to remove the selected text, picture or object.

Cut command – Copies the data to the Clipboard (a virtual, temporary holding area). The data will be deleted from its original location as soon as you 'paste' it somewhere else. Pasting cut data moves the data from its original location.

Deleted Items – This folder holds e-mail you've deleted.

Desktop folder – This folder contains links to items on your Desktop.

Documents folder – This folder contains documents you've saved, subfolders you created and folders created by Windows 7, including My Stationary, Contacts, My Music and more.

Domain name – For our use here, a domain name is synonymous with a website name.

Downloaded program files – Files that are download automatically when you view certain web pages. They are stored temporarily in a folder on your hard disk, and accessed when and if needed.

Downloads folder – This folder does not contain anything by default. It does offer a place to save items you download from the Internet, like drivers and third-party programs.

Dialogue box – A place to make changes to default settings in an application. Clicking File and then Print, for instance, opens the Print dialogue box where you can configure the type of paper you're using, select a printer, and more.

Disk Cleanup – An application included with Windows 7 that offers a safe and effective way to reduce unnecessary data on your PC. With Disk Cleanup you can remove temporary files, empty the Recycle Bin, remove set-up log files, and downloaded program files (among other things), all in a single process.

Disk Defragmenter – An application included with Windows 7 that analyses the data stored on your hard drive and consolidates files that are not stored together. This enhances performance by making data on your hard drive work faster by making it easier to access. Disk Defragmenter runs automatically, once a week, in the middle of the night.

DPI – Dots per inch refers to how many dots (or pixels) per inch are on a computer monitor.

Drafts – This folder holds e-mail messages you've started and then saved, but not yet completed and sent.

Driver – A driver is a piece of software (or code) that allows the device to communicate with Windows 7 and vice versa.

DV – Digital video, generally used as DV camera.

E-mail address – A virtual address you use for sending and receiving e-mail. It often takes this form: *yourname@yourispname.com*.

Ethernet – A technology that uses Ethernet cables to transmit data and network computers.

Ethernet cable – A cable that is used to connect PCs to routers and cable modems, among other things.

Favourite – A web page that you've chosen to maintain a shortcut for in the Favorites Center.

Favorites Center – This folder contains the items in Internet Explorer's Favorites list. It may also include folders created by the computer manufacturer or Microsoft, including Links, Microsoft Websites and MSN Websites.

Flash drive – A small portable device that is used for quick backups of data or ReadyBoost. Flash drives are often referred to as thumb drives and plug into an available USB port.

Flip and Flip 3D – A way to move through open windows graphically instead of clicking the item on the Taskbar.

Form data – In Internet Explorer, this is information that's been saved using the Internet Explorer's autocomplete form data functionality. If you don't want forms to be filled out automatically by you or someone else who has access to your PC and user account, delete this.

Formatting toolbar – A toolbar in an application window that often sits just below a standard toolbar and offers drop-down lists for the font, font size and language, as well as options to configure the font (or any selected text) as bold, italic or underlined. There's often a Color option for assigning a colour to a font too, as well as alignment tools for Align Left, Center, Align Right, and finally Bullets.

Gadget – In our terms, an icon on the Sidebar like the Weather or Clock gadget.

GHz – Short for gigahertz, this term describes how fast a processor can work. One GHz equals 1 billion cycles per second, so a 2.4 GHz computer chip will execute calculations at 240 billion cycles per second. It's only important to know that the faster the chip, the faster the PC.

GPU – Short for graphics processing unit, it's a processor used specifically for rendering graphics. Having a processor just for graphics frees up the main CPU (central processing unit), allowing it to work faster on other tasks.

History – In Internet Explorer, this is the list of websites you've visited and any web addresses you've typed. Anyone who has access to your PC and user account can look at your History list to see where you've been.

Home page – The web page that opens when you open IE8. You can set the home page and configure additional pages to open as well.

Hotspot – A wi-fi hotspot lets you connect to the Internet without having to be tethered to an Ethernet cable or tied down with a high monthly wireless bill. Sometimes this service is free, provided you have the required wireless hardware.

Icon – A visual representation of a file or folder that you can click to open.

Inbox – This folder holds e-mail you've received.

Instant messaging (IM) – Text and instant messaging require you to type your message and click a Send button. It's similar to e-mail, but it's instantaneous; the recipient gets the message right after you send it. Instant messaging is the term generally reserved for text communications between two or more computers; text messaging is a term generally reserved for communicating between two mobile phones.

Interface – What you see on the screen when working in a window. In Paint's interface, you see the Menu bar, Toolbox and Color box.

Internet – A large web of computers that communicate via land lines, satellite and cable for the purpose of sharing information and data. Also called the World Wide Web.

Internet server – A computer that stores data off site. Windows Live Mail offers Internet servers to hold e-mail and data, so that you do not have to store this on your PC. Internet servers allow you to access information from any computer that can access the internet.

ISP – Internet Service Provider. A company that provides internet access, usually for a fee.

Junk e-mail – This folder holds e-mail that Windows Live Mail thinks is spam. You should check this folder occasionally, since Mail may put e-mail in there you want to read.

Link – A shortcut to a web page. Links are often offered in an e-mail, document or web page to allow you to access a site without having to actually type in its name. In almost all instances, links are underlined and in a different colour than the text on the rest of the page.

Links folder – This folder contains shortcuts to the Desktop, Downloads, Recent Places, and more.

Load – A web page must 'load' before you can access it. Some pages load instantly while others take a few seconds.

Magnifier – A tool in the Ease of Access suite of applications. You use Magnifier to drastically increase the size of the information shown on the screen.

Mail server – A computer that your ISP configures to allow you to send and receive e-mail. It often includes a POP3 incoming mail server and an SMTP outgoing mail server. Often the server names look something like *pop.yourispnamehere.com* and *smtp.yourispnamehere.com*.

Malware – stands for malicious software. Malware includes viruses, worms, spyware, etc.

Menu – A title on the Menu bar (such as File, Edit, View). Clicking a menu name opens a drop-down list with additional choices (Open, Save, Print).

Menu bar – A bar that runs across the top of an application that offers menus. Often, these menus include File, Edit, View, Insert, Format and Help.

Music folder – This folder contains sample music and music you save to the PC.

Narrator – A basic screen reader included with Windows 7. This application will read text that appears on the screen to you, while you navigate using the keyboard and mouse.

Navigate – The process of moving from one web page to another or viewing items on a single web page. Often the term is used as follows 'click the link to navigate to the new web page'.

Network – A group of computers, printers and other devices that communicate wirelessly or through wired connections.

Network adapter – A piece of hardware that lets your computer connect to a network, such as the Internet or a local network.

Network Discovery – A state where computers can find other computers on the network. Network Discovery must be on to locate and communicate with network devices.

Network and Sharing Center – A collection of features where you can easily access network connections, sharing options, networked computers and devices, and diagnose and repair features.

Network map – The Network map details each of your network connections graphically, and allows you to distinguish easily among wired, wireless and Internet connections.

Network window – The Network window offers links to computers on your network and the Network and Sharing Center. You can also add printers and wireless devices here.

Newsgroup – An online forum where you can share ideas, post opinions, get help and meet other people with interests similar to your own.

Notification area – The area of the Taskbar that includes the clock and the volume icons, and also holds icons for applications that are running in the background. You may see icons for your anti-virus software, music players, updates or Windows security alerts.

Offline web pages – These are web pages you choose to store on your computer so you can view them without being connected to the Internet. Upon connection, the data is synchronised.

Operating system – In this case, the operating system is Windows 7. This is what allows you to operate your computer's *system*. You will use Windows 7 to find things you have stored on your computer, connect to the Internet, send and receive e-mail, and surf the web, among other things.

Outbox – This folder holds e-mail you've written but have not yet sent.

Page Setup button – Clicking Page Setup opens the Page Setup dialogue box. Here you can select a paper size, source, and create headers and footers. You can also change orientation and margins, all of which is dependent on what features your printer supports.

Parental controls – If you have children or grandchildren, or even a forgetful or scatterbrained partner who needs imposed computer limitations, you can apply them using parental controls. With these controls you are in charge of the hours a user can access the computer, which games they can play and what programs they can run (among other things).

Partition – A hard drive has a certain amount of space to store data, sometimes 40 GB, 80 GB, 120 GB, or more. Often, people or computer manufacturers separate this space into two or three distinct spaces, called partitions, drives or volumes. One partition may contain system files, one may contain program files and the other may contain data.

Paste command – Copies or moves cut or copied data to the new location. If the data was cut, it will be moved. If the data was copied, it will be copied.

Permissions – Rules associated with a shared resource, like a folder, file or printer, that define who can use a resource and what they can do once they have access to it.

Phishing – A technique used by computer hackers to get you to divulge personal information like bank account numbers. Phishing filters warn you of potential phishing websites and e-mails, and are included in Windows 7. In other words, an attempt by an unscrupulous website or hacker to obtain personal data, including but not limited to bank account numbers, National Insurance numbers and e-mail addresses.

Pictures folder – This folder contains sample pictures and pictures you save to the PC.

Pixel -The smallest unit for data displayed on a computer. Resolution is defined by how many pixels you choose to display.

Playlist – A group of songs that you can save and then listen to as a group, burn to a CD, copy to a portable music player, and more.

Podcast – An online broadcast, like a radio show.

POP3 server name – The name of the computer that you will use to get your e-mail from your ISP. Your ISP will give you this information when you subscribe.

Power plan – A group of settings that you can configure to tell Windows 7 when and if to turn off the computer monitor or display, and when or if to put the computer to sleep.

Processor – Short for microprocessor, it's the silicon chip that contains the central processing unit (CPU) inside a computer. Generally, the terms CPU and processor are used interchangeably. A CPU does almost all of the computer's calculations and is the most important piece of hardware in a computer system.

Print button – Clicking Print opens the Print dialogue box where you can configure the page range, select a printer, change page orientation, change print order and choose a paper type. Additional options include print quality, output bins, and more. Of course, the choices offered depend on what your printer offers. If your printer can only print at 300 x 300 dots per inch, you can't configure it to print at a higher quality.

Print Preview button – Clicking Print Preview opens a window where you can see before you print what the printout will actually look like. You can switch between portrait and landscape views, access the Page Setup dialogue box, and more.

Programs – See Applications.

Public folder – Folders where you can share data. Anyone with an account on the computer can access the data inside these folders. You can also configure the Public folder to share files with people using other computers on your local network.

Publish – In Windows Calendar, a way to distribute a calendar electronically so that it is shared with others. The calendar can be shared via an online source like a web page or on the user's own network.

RAM – Short for random access memory, it's the hardware inside your computer that temporarily stores data that is being used by the operating system or programs. Although there are many types of RAM, all you need to know is that the more RAM you have, the faster your computer will (theoretically) run and perform.

ReadyBoost – A new technology that lets you add more RAM (random access memory) to a PC using a USB flash drive or a secure digital memory card (like the one in your digital camera), as RAM, if it meets certain requirements. Just plug the device into an open slot on your PC and, if it is compatible, choose to use the device as RAM.

Recycle Bin – The Recycle Bin holds deleted files until you decide to empty it. The Recycle Bin serves as a safeguard, allowing you to recover items accidentally deleted or items you thought you no longer wanted but later decide you need. Note that once you empty the Recycle Bin, the items in it are gone forever.

Registration – A non-mandatory task that you generally perform during the Windows 7 activation process. By registering you can get e-mails regarding new products and help. Registration is not mandatory.

Remote Desktop Connection – A Windows 7 program you can use to access your computer from somewhere else, like an office or hotel room.

Resolution – How many pixels are shown on a computer screen. Choosing 800 by 600 pixels means that the Desktop is shown to you with 800 pixels across and 600 pixels down. When you increase the resolution, you increase the number of pixels on the screen.

Rip – A term used to describe the process of copying files from a physical CD to your hard drive, and thus your music library.

Router – A piece of equipment used to send data from computer to computer on a network. A router 'routes' the data to the correct PC and also rejects data that is harmful or from unknown sources.

RSS – A new way to access information on the Internet. Also called Really Simple Syndication (and occasionally Rich Site Summary), you can use this technology to 'subscribe' to RSS data, and the information or website you subscribe to will be updated automatically on your PC, and will only acquire information you've yet to view.

Screensaver – A screensaver is a picture or animation that covers your screen and appears after your computer has been idle for a specific amount of time that you set. You can configure your screensaver to require a password on waking up for extra security.

Scroll up and scroll down – A process of using the scroll bars on a web page or the arrow keys on a keyboard to move up and down the pages of a website or to navigate through open windows.

Sent Items – This folder stores copies of e-mail messages you've sent.

Setup Log Files – Files created by Windows during set-up processes.

Sidebar – The Sidebar is a Desktop component that lies *on top of* the Desktop. It's transparent and offers, by default, a calendar, the weather and a clock. You can delete and add Sidebar items, called gadgets, to show the information you want to see. You can also hide the Sidebar.

SMTP server name – The name of the computer that you will use to send e-mail using your ISP. Your ISP will give you this information when you subscribe.

Snipping Tool – A feature in Windows 7 that allows you to drag your cursor around any area on the screen to copy and capture it. Once captured, you can save it, edit it and/or send it to an e-mail recipient.

Sound Recorder – A simple tool included with Windows 7 with only three options: Start recording, Stop recording and Resume recording. You can save recorded clips as notes to yourself or insert them into movies or slide shows.

Spam – Unwanted e-mail. Compare spam to junk faxes or junk postal mail.

Speech Recognition – A program included with Windows 7. This program does a good job of allowing you to control your computer with your voice. From the speech recognition options you can set up your microphone, take a speech tutorial, train your computer to better understand you, and more.

Standard toolbar – A toolbar that is often underneath a Menu bar (in an application window) that contains icons, or pictures, of common commands. Common commands include New, Open, Save, Print, Print Preview, Find, Cut, Copy, Paste, Undo, and Date/Time.

Status bar – A toolbar that often appears at the bottom of an application window and offers information about what you are doing at the moment. If you aren't doing anything, it often offers the helpful words 'For Help, press F1', otherwise it offers information regarding the tool you've selected from a toolbar or information about the task you're performing.

Sticky Keys – This setting allows you to configure the keyboard so that you never have to press three keys at once (such as when you must press the CTRL, ALT and DELETE keys together to log on to Windows). With Sticky Keys, you can use one key to perform these tasks. You configure the key to use for three-key tasks.

Subfolder – A folder inside another folder.

Subscribe – Using Windows Calendar, a method used to access a calendar created by someone else. The calendar is displayed in

Windows Calendar and is updated automatically as changes are made to the original. You can choose how often to update the calendar.

Sync – The process of comparing data in one location to the data in another, and performing tasks to match it up. If data has been added or deleted from one device, for instance, synching can also add or delete it from the other.

Sync Center – An application included with Windows 7 that helps you keep your files, music, contacts, pictures and other data in sync between your computer and mobile devices, network files and folders, and compatible programs such as Outlook. Technically, syncing is the process of keeping files matched, when those files are used on more than one device.

System Restore – If enabled, stores 'restore points' on your PC's hard drive. If something goes wrong you can run System Restore, choose one of these points and revert to a pre-problem date. Since System Restore only deals with 'system data', none of your personal data will be affected (not even your last e-mail).

System Restore Point – A snapshot of the computer that Windows 7 keeps in case something happens and you need to revert to it, because of a bad installation or hardware driver.

Tags – Data about a particular piece of data, like a photo or a song or album. Tags can be used to group pictures or music in various ways. Some tags are applied automatically when you import pictures from a digital camera, including the date they were uploaded, along with any name you applied to the imported group. You can also create your own tags.

Taskbar – The bar that runs horizontally across the bottom of the Windows 7 interface and contains the Start button, Quick Launch area and Notification area. It also offers a place to view and access open files, folders and applications.

Temporary files – Files created and stored by programs for use by the program. Most of these temporary files are deleted when you exit the program, but some do remain.

Temporary Internet files – Files that contain copies of web pages you've visited on your hard drive, so that you can view the pages more quickly when visiting them again.

Text messaging – Text and instant messaging (IM) require you to type your message and click a Send button. It's similar to e-mail, but it's instantaneous; the recipient gets the message right after you send it. Instant messaging is the term generally reserved for text communications between two or more computers; text messaging is a term generally reserved for communicating between two mobile phones.

Thumbnails – Small icons of your pictures, videos and documents. Thumbnails will be recreated as needed should you choose to delete them using Disk Cleanup.

Transition – A segue when moving from one picture to another in a slide show, such as fading in or out.

URL – This stands for Uniform Resource Locator and denotes a location on a network, either the Internet or a local network.

USB – Universal Serial Bus, a standard for transmitting data between an external device to a computer. There are all kinds of USB devices, including mice, keyboards, flash drives, printers, cameras and backup devices. USB devices are plug-and-play, and thus, easy to install.

Video messaging – A form of instant messaging where one or both users also offer live video of themselves during the conversation.

Videos folder – This folder contains sample videos and videos you save to the PC.

Video format – The video file type, such as AVI or WMA.

Virus – A self-replicating program that infects computers with intent to do harm. Viruses often come in the form of an attachment in an e-mail.

Visualisations – Produced by Windows 7 and Windows Media Player, these are graphical representations of the music you play.

Web browser – Windows 7 comes with Internet Explorer, an application you can use to explore the Internet. Internet Explorer lets you 'surf the web', and it has everything you need, including a pop-up blocker, zoom settings and accessibility options, as well as tools you can use to save your favourite web pages, set home pages and sign up for read RSS feeds.

Webcam – A camera that can send live images over the Internet.

Website – A group of web pages that contain related information. Microsoft's website contains information about Microsoft products, for instance.

Window – When you open a program from the Start menu, a document, folder or a picture, it opens in a 'window'. Window, as it's used in this context, is synonymous with an open program, file or folder and has nothing to do with the word Windows, used with Windows 7.

Windows Calendar – A full-featured calendar application included in Windows 7 that lets you manage your own affairs as well as the affairs of others, using a familiar calendar interface.

Windows Defender – You don't have to do much to Windows Defender except understand that it offers protection against Internet threats. It's enabled by default and it runs in the background. However, if you ever think your computer has been attacked by an Internet threat (virus, worm, malware, etc.) you can run a manual scan here.

Windows Firewall – If enabled and configured properly, the firewall will help prevent hackers (people whose job it is to get into your computer and do harm to it) from accessing your PC and data. The firewall blocks most programs from communicating outside the network (or outside your PC). If you want to allow a program to communicate outside your safety zone you can 'allow' a program by adding it to an 'exceptions' list. This is all very easy to do.

Windows Media Center – An application that allows you to watch, pause and record live television, locate, download and/or listen to music and radio, view, edit and share photos and videos, and play DVDs (among other things).

Windows Mobility Center – An application that lets you adjust your mobile PC, tablet PC or laptop computer settings quickly, including things like volume, wireless and brightness.

Windows Update – If enabled and configured properly, when you are online, Windows 7 will check for security updates automatically and install them. You don't have to do anything, and your PC is always updated with the latest security patches and features.

Worm – A self-replicating program that infects computers with intent to do harm. However, unlike a virus, it does not need to attach itself to a running program.

Troubleshooting guide

12. Networking